THE LATER MIDDLE AGES

IS VOLUME

77

OF THE

Twentieth Century Encyclopedia of Catholicism

UNDER SECTION

VII

THE HISTORY OF THE CHURCH

IT IS ALSO THE

44TH

VOLUME IN ORDER OF PUBLICATION

Edited by HENRI DANIEL-ROPS of the Académie Française

THE LATER MIDDLE AGES

By BERNARD GUILLEMAIN

Translated from the French by S. TAYLOR

HAWTHORN BOOKS · PUBLISHERS · *New York*

First Edition, June, 1960
Second Printing, June, 1963

NIHIL OBSTAT

Adrianus van Vliet, S.T.D.

   Censor Deputatus

IMPRIMATUR

E. Morrogh Bernard

   Vicarius Generalis

Westmonasterii, die I APRILIS MCMLX

H-9468

CONTENTS

PART I

PRELUDE TO DISINTEGRATION

There are impressive grounds for thinking that Christendom reached its high-water mark between the end of the twelfth century and the final third of the thirteenth. There is the picture of Innocent III, with the pallium about his neck and the tiara on his head, speeding knights on their way to crush the heretics, making and unmaking the sovereigns of Germany, receiving a vassal's homage from John of England. There is St Francis of Assisi, singing the praises of the Lady Poverty, his call bringing men in their thousands to don the habit of coarse cloth, his influence putting more of tenderness and of love into art and poetry. There is the University of Paris, watering the West with its "river of sapience" or, to use the formula of another pope, "baking the intellectual bread [of Christendom] in its oven". There is St Thomas Aquinas bringing reason and faith into harmony and raising as his monument the *Summa Theologica*. And everywhere, there are the Gothic cathedrals, their spires pointing skywards, imprisoning the light in their stained glass windows, bending inventive genius and technical skill to the glory of God.

But we must not be misled by these triumphs. Their brightness is contained within a shadowy framework. Whether we look to the faith, the primacy and purity of which formed the keystone of a Christian civilization; or to the Church, insisting on her autonomy so as not to be torn between the conflicting demands of temporal powers; or to the papacy, which arrogated to itself supreme authority over society—whichever way we look, the elements defining Roman Christendom were continually disputed. It will be our task to understand this perpetual questioning.

But although our subject may be confined to evoking the vicissitudes in the unity, meaning and form of the organic community formed by the Christians of the West, we cannot forget that at this very moment men were being subjected to the pull of other loyalties and other interests than those of Christianity. Through the towns, through the merchants' associations and through the transfer of funds between the Low Countries and Italy, between the North Sea ports and those of the Baltic or Mediterranean, along the Rhine and the sea-routes, in the great fairs of Champagne, thanks to the Lombards and the "Cahorsins", a new network of relations was taking shape; its object was the search for profit; its values went by the name of cloth, spices and wine; warehouses, guild lodges, market-places, money-changers' tables—these were its staging points; its frontiers extended to the Muslim ports along the whole northern coast of Africa, and to the trading posts of the Greek territories and the Crimea where, in their turn, they linked up with the caravan routes to the Sudan, the Persian Gulf, Iraq, Turkestan, the Russian steppes and the Far East. The history of this commercial civilization cuts across and sometimes influences the one we are concerned with but, basically, it is quite different—and that, assuredly, indicates a remarkable lack of cohesion in the very age when Christianity appeared to be bearing its finest fruits.

CHAPTER I

THE CHURCH IN THE THIRTEENTH CENTURY

During the second and third quarters of the thirteenth century canon law reached its high-water mark. Five small collections of pontifical decisions (*decretals*) had been added to the *Decretum* of Gratian. In 1234 Gregory IX, feeling the need for a fresh code, replaced all former collections by a single one in five volumes—the *Five Books of Decretals*—which, addressed to Bologna, was to supply the material for a series of commentaries that went to make up the classical juridical doctrine of the Church. Canon law stood, unified, pontifical, complete: it defined the structure of the ecclesiastical body, the rules which Christians must obey in their moral and social activities, as well as the relations of the spiritual power with the world. In what measure did this harmonious theoretical construction influence historical development, and was it in turn influenced by history? These are the questions that we must now try to evaluate.

THE POSITION OF THE PAPACY

The most striking feature of the Church's constitution was the place occupied in it by the papacy. It was recognized that the Church of Rome, in the person of its bishop, exercised all the powers and privileges Christ had promised his Church, that the other Churches occupied a subordinate position, that the one was the head and the others the members. St Peter's successor legislated for the Church universal: it was his decisions

that enriched canon law; he granted dispensations, he reserved
to himself the right to release the faithful from the sentences of
excommunication or interdict that they might have automatic-
ally incurred, by reason of specified acts; he alone, in a certain
number of cases, administered the sacrament of penance, and
to help him in the exercise of this spiritual function he created
the Apostolic Penitentiary. As for ecclesiastical lawsuits,
whether in the first instance or on appeal, he examined them in
the consistory, surrounded by his cardinals, but it happened
with increasing frequency that he had to rely on a cardinal or
chaplains to draw up the judgement. As head of the ecclesiastical hierarchy, he confirmed, or took the initiative in directly
nominating, prelates, although the ancient principle of election
to sees and abbeys still stood; he recommended to collators
the candidates he hoped to see endowed with benefices, who
were thus provided, through his good offices, with grants in
expectation. Clement IV, in 1265, posited the principle that, as
absolute master of the Church instituted by Christ himself, he
had the complete disposal of all benefices; and in fact he did
pronounce a growing number of particular or general "reservations". This seizure of Church offices allowed him to augment
his financial resources: taking a third of the annual income as
servitia communia from major benefices, or the first year's
income as annates from minor livings, he laid a tax on the
benefices at his disposal. The duties of his chancellery demanded a highly qualified and numerous staff; his treasury, the
Camera Apostolica, having long administered a modest budget,
became an exchequer whose head, the chamberlain, had an
important part to play; the collection of taxes from the lands of
Christendom, the transfer, the clearing or the distant assignment
of funds all called for the services of Italian bankers. When
added to the links that the Holy See had contrived to multiply
and strengthen between itself and the various institutions of
the Church, its policy in regard to benefices and finance was a
decided reinforcement of its work of centralization.

THE CONCERN WITH REFORM

Under the grip of the Sovereign Pontiff, however, the Church was not muted. Without her providential mission being called in question, criticisms of her present state were formulated and new schemes outlined; she was informed by an abiding concern for amendment and enrichment which, not without resistance, and occasional outbursts, gave her new aspects.

Not all canonists were agreed on the definition of papal authority. The celebrated Henry of Susa, known under the name of Hostiensis because he was Cardinal Bishop of Ostia, saw in the pope no more than an agent having power of attorney and, likening the Church to a corporation, he concluded that authority is divided between the head and the members and lies, in the last resort, with the community of the faithful if its organs fail.

From the middle of the century vigorous protests were raised against the attitude of the popes: their requests for contributions to support their temporal enterprises, their interference in the choice of holders of benefices and their nepotism all aroused growing disapproval; at the same time, indignation was prevalent that the intrigues of the cardinals should keep the Apostolic See vacant for long months—it was even necessary for the electors to be locked in the bishop's palace at Viterbo, subjected to the inclemency of the elements by removal of the roof, and reduced to bread and water, before Gregory X could succeed Clement IV in 1271 after an interregnum of nearly three years.

The moral reform of the clergy needed continual attention; complaints concerned their love of money, moral lapses and lukewarmness in religious matters; the evil of absenteeism was spreading inside the chapters: the prebend was looked on as an annuity, the canon drawing it while exempting himself from the accomplishment of his religious duties; if he was a teacher, or a king's counsellor, or an official of the Roman court, he would not rest until he had collected several such posts to swell his income. The ignorance of the minor clergy called forth the barbs of the writers. The register of Eudes II Rigaud, Bishop of Rouen from 1247 to 1276, contains a list of these ills; it precludes any exaggeration, restricting to four per cent of priests examined the number guilty of sexual disorders; but it leaves an impression of inferior ability.

In 1274, the ecumenical council of Lyons dwelt on disorders of all kinds: it tried to put a halt to the abuses of pontifical practice by recalling the traditional prescriptions of canon law in the matter of ecclesiastical recruitment; it prohibited the plurality of benefices and laid down strict rules for the holding of conclaves. The effect of these sensible provisions proved to be slight.

In actual fact, the need for reform was expressed not so much in admonitions and juridical texts as in the creation of new institutions. When the monastic revival took place at the end of the eleventh and the beginning of the twelfth century, Cluny had not been found wanting; in the same way, Cîteaux and Prémontré were not affected by the thirteenth-century decadence—in fact the total of the provincial houses of the great Burgundian monastery rose from 530 to 694. But the ideal had declined; the direct economic exploitation of the land by the monks and lay brothers had gradually given way to the traditional working of large estates. The rural form of Benedictine monasticism was no longer appropriate to men, often from urban backgrounds, in search of an austere and exalting spirituality.

THE MENDICANT ORDERS

The intentions of Dominic Guzman and Francesco Bernardone differed from one another. The Spaniard, who was a member of the clergy, wished to spread the truth, after taking great pains to instruct himself in it, while at the same time practising poverty so as to give added weight to his teaching; when the crusaders had conquered the lands of the barons in the south of France who were suspected of heresy, the Bishop of Toulouse took Dominic and his six companions into his service to help him proclaim sound doctrine in his diocese. But Dominic's firm intention was to spread to the whole of Christendom the mission of his small team of preachers. It was doubtless with this in mind that Innocent III had it decreed by the council that bishops who thought it appropriate might surround themselves with clerks fitted "to take charge of preaching, hear confessions, distribute penances and do all things ordained for the salvation of souls". Dominic then chose the rule of St Augustine to direct the spiritual life of his companions and saw to the adoption of the "customs" which so ordered conventual life that the preacher might give himself up to intensive study "by night and day, at home or while travelling". On December 22nd, 1216, Pope Honorius III, with remarkable boldness, took the group of sixteen friars in Toulouse under his protection, raised it to the status of an "Order" and defined its rôle in the manner in which its founder had from the first envisaged it: "Considering that the brothers of your Order must be the champions of the faith and the true light of the world, we confirm your Order and take it under our government." Dominic thereupon began to disperse the friars; within a few years the Preachers were established in the centre of heresy at Toulouse, in the Christian capital of Rome and in the university towns of Paris and Bologna; they were scattered thickly throughout France, Spain and Italy, and reached as far as Poland. The results of the experiment were conclusive: the "constitutions" of 1220 organized the Order by combining the authority of the superiors with representation of all the friars within the chapters. Eight provinces were established, including that of England, followed by four new ones in the Holy Land, Greece, Poland and Scandinavia (or Dacia). By the end of the thirteenth century more than 400 monasteries were to house some ten thousand Dominicans.

Quite different was the development of the Friars Minor. The son of a cloth merchant of Assisi, Francis had resolved to sacrifice everything to "the Lady Poverty", whom he espoused;

his life of renunciation was to enable him to set an example
of complete independence with regard to worldly goods, the
pure joy of a child of God who had need "neither of gold nor
silver nor coin, nor of any scrip, nor of two coats, nor of
shoes, nor of staffs"; and to allow him to announce in the
rigour of the letter, to the lay society of the time, the precepts
of the Gospel. But his message, avidly received by minds given
to mysticism, ran the risk of engendering anarchy in the form
of little groups, leaderless and unattached, which would end
up by inventing their own truth. Put on his guard by the
reserve of the bishops, Francis himself comprehended the danger. He did not regard himself as a natural organizer, so he
had recourse to the pope and Innocent III took him under his
wing. From this point, a sort of dissociation set in: the pauper
of Assisi thought of nothing but his apostolate; as early as
1217 he provided for eleven provinces for his congregation,
whose numbers were swelling in a spectacular manner; he
wanted to spread the word of Christ in North Africa; un-
daunted by setbacks that cost some of his companions their
lives, he sent out further missions in 1219; he attached himself
to the crusaders and confronted the Sultan of Egypt. At the
same time, between 1220 and 1223, the pope transformed the
lay brotherhoods into a religious order: the rule of 1223 certainly evoked the poverty and charity that were indispensable,
but it erected a hierarchy, provided for chapters and established
a cardinal-protector. Francis gave his approval, but it was in
solitude that he spent the last two years of his life, giving himself up to extraordinary acts of mortification, being marked
by the stigmata, singing a hymn to the sun and exalting poverty
in his spiritual testament.

The two mendicant Orders now gathered their forces together. But while the one had no difficulty in accepting the
grouping of its members in urban monasteries—which became
so many schools—the building of churches, the receipt of tithes
and gifts (excluding real estate), the other went through a long
and painful period of re-appraisal. To agree to accommodations

was surely to betray the founder's design? The sole rule of
anyone claiming to be "Franciscan" was surely to conform to
the words, the deeds and above all the writings of St Francis?
This was the view of the "Spirituals", or "zealots", who from
the beginning were opposed to the accommodaters, the "Con-
ventuals". The cardinal issue concerned the way in which
poverty should be understood. It was the Holy See that resolved the matter: in 1230, Gregory IX distinguished property,
which remained formally condemned, from its use, which might
be tolerated; he decided therefore that religious and monastic
buildings should continue to belong to their donors but that
the Friars Minor should enjoy the use of them, and that they
should be able to use money on condition that they spent it
through an intermediary and deposited it, outside their houses,
with a trustworthy person. In 1245, Innocent IV declared that
all the movable property held by the Franciscans should belong
to the Holy See, and that the procurators instituted by his
predecessor should carry out all financial transactions. This
juridical compromise, many times revised, was scarcely calculated to slake the thirst of impassioned souls.

These grave differences of opinion did not, however, compromise either the success of the Friars Minor or the spreading
influence of the new Orders. In 1263, there were twenty-five to
thirty thousand disciples of St Francis spread over eleven hundred and thirty houses in thirty-two provinces. But figures at
best can give only an incomplete picture of the influence of
the Mendicants. It was manifested in countless ways. It
amounted to a fresh upsurge of monasticism, adding to its
liturgical, rural, Benedictine forms new, town-based ones, engaged in teaching and missionary activity, with such orders as
the Carmelites, the Hermits of St Augustine and the Order of
Servites. It was marked, too, by the appearance of women's
Orders, the most famous of which was the Poor Ladies whose
founder, St Clare, had been installed by St Francis in the
hermitage of San Damiano, below the town of Assisi; as well
as by the revival of charitable congregations devoted to the

ransom of captives, the reception of repentant prostitutes, the care of the sick and infirm; and likewise the setting-up of lay associations, the Third Orders within which men and women, while remaining in the world, committed themselves to a life stripped of luxuries, to reciting the canonical hours and visiting the poor. These developments constituted so many contributions to the sensibility, the piety, the culture and the artistic inspiration of the age.

THE MISSIONS

The mendicant Orders not only infused new blood into the body of Christendom, they also turned their energies to bringing it new members. Peaceable preaching to the unbeliever went back to the very origins of the Church, with the directions of its divine founder; nevertheless, from the time of Charlemagne, evangelization seemed to have taken a second place to conquest or occupation: in Saxony, and later beyond the Elbe among the Slavs, it was the sword that carved a way for the Bible. In northern and central Europe, the conversion of the princes—often from interested motives—was gradually followed by that of their subjects. Christian acquisitions at the expense of Islam had involved the subjection of infidel communities, but no systematic attempt at conversion had been made. Having acquired political cohesion, western Christendom first made use of temporal methods, ranging from extermination to tolerance; the government of territory and bodies had taken precedence over the winning of souls.

But this was the prize that St Dominic and St Francis hoped to gain. The Spaniard had had in mind the Kumans of southern Russia; the Italian would not rest until he had made contact with the Muslim: in 1219 he succeeded in speaking before the Sultan of Egypt, when he offered to walk on burning coals; he sent a handful of his companions along the coast of North Africa, but these messengers of the Gospel were ill-advised enough to deride Mohammed and the Koran, and in 1220 they were killed in Marrakesh

The Islamic bloc remained intact: the bishopric that had been founded in Morocco did no more than provide for the worship of the sultan's Christian militia, and from the middle of the thirteenth century the bishop resigned himself to living for most of his time at Seville, which was his parent see; the provinces of the two mendicant Orders in the Holy Land experienced difficulties that increased with the reduction in size of the Latin bridgehead; but the Franciscans hung on in Jerusalem, and won the right to guard the Holy Sepulchre.

It was the advance of the Mongols which, paradoxically, opened up an immense new missionary field. Masters of Mongolia, bidding fair to dominate China, Tibet, Turkestan and Iran, Genghis Khan's successors had launched their horsemen in the direction of the West, a minor peninsula not yet absorbed into their empire. In 1241, an army had crossed central Europe as far as Moravia; another one had advanced up to the Adriatic coast. The German and Polish knights who had been the first to bar the invaders' path had been swept aside; a stouter defence was slowly beginning to take shape, when the Mongols became preoccupied with the succession of their supreme head, the great khan, and withdrew, not without wreaking havoc in Serbia and Bulgaria. The danger might reappear at any time; the yellow-skinned conquerors were in control of southern Russia, where they had established a khanate. For all that, the traders who had been in touch with the Tartars reported them to be tolerant and inquiring; they said that, among the religions they had encountered, the heathens seemed to look with a certain favour upon Nestorian Christianity; and it was a fact that these amazing heretical churches were proliferating anew, right out to the Far East, and were providing the Mongol princes with counsellors and merchants. The idea that the legendary kingdom of Prester John was possibly situated somewhere in Tartar territory was the final element in changing terror to missionary fervour. Innocent IV, in 1245, dispatched the Franciscan, John of Pian del Carpine, on an exploratory mission. And as Louis IX of France, who was at that moment mounting an attack on Egypt, received Mongol envoys who were themselves interested in the fight against Islam in the Near East, he sent off a mission of Dominicans in his turn for the great khan's capital. The replies were couched in uncompromising terms: the Tartars demanded submission from the princes of the West, but the monks who brought the letters confirmed that the Asiatics were favourably disposed and that Christian communities existed in their empire.

In the northern ports of the Black Sea where there were Italian merchants, in Armenia and Georgia, and in northern Iran, which was regularly visited by merchants and where Christians of several different rites subsisted, Franciscans and Dominicans established themselves; they followed in the wake of caravans; they founded small centres of evangelization; John of Monte Corvino crossed Persia and India and, after nine years of travelling, arrived in 1298 in China, the "Cathay" whither he had been preceded by the Venetian trader Marco Polo: at Pekin (Kambalik) he founded a church which grew rapidly in numbers.

Method was introduced. The general chapter of the Order of Preachers called for the teaching of Hebrew and Arabic in certain monasteries. Its third Master General, St Raymond of Peñaforte, directed St Thomas Aquinas to write his *Summa contra Gentiles* and advised the Spanish kings to create colleges at Murcia and Tunis. The Catalan Raymond Lull, having entered the Franciscan Third Order, decided about the year 1266 to devote himself to the conversion of the Mohammedans; he learned Arabic, and he imagined a combination of arguments, which he called the *Ars magna*, to overcome all objections and convince his adversaries; he persuaded the King of Minorca to set up a college at Miramar for thirteen Friars Minor; he himself set the example, first among the schismatics of Cilicia and later in North Africa.

As a result of the missionaries' work, the Church came to realize again perhaps that it was not bound fast to one civilization and one political situation, those of Roman Christendom.

The teams of mendicant friars, much too small for the job they had to do and doubtless misunderstood by the majority of the clergy, were giving it a new dimension.

THE INQUISITION

The immediate problem of the search for heretics was a more pressing preoccupation. Were they not, to use Innocent III's comparison, committing a crime analogous to that of high treason, the penalty for which in Roman law was death?

The bishops or their representatives were responsible for visiting their parishes and choosing, in each of them, a certain number of the faithful, whose lives were above reproach, to point out suspects. Since Catharism was still strong in Languedoc, despite the military expeditions, these occasional testifiers were transformed into permanent informers; a priest was assigned to them so that, wherever the menace of heresy might manifest itself, the ecclesiastical authorities should be immediately and constantly alerted. The kings of France, as well as Emperor Frederick II and the Senator of Rome, undertook to put their agents at the Church's disposal and to punish without indulgence those convicted of heresy; the Count of Toulouse, as a condition of being allowed to resume possession of some of his lands, promised in 1229 to pay a bounty to whoever should apprehend a proved heretic.

But the system either showed itself to be inadequate—this was the case in the south of France—or else lent itself to violence and ill-timed actions. In an apostolic constitution of February, 1231, Gregory IX enumerated the battery of sanctions which the Roman Church had the right to use against the opponents of its faith; and, while reserving the authority of the bishops, in a series of measures covering successively Germany, Italy, Aragon, northern and southern France, he handed over to the Friars Preachers the responsibility for seeking out and judging heretics.

A complete change of methods followed: in the northern part of France, Robert le Bougre, a former Cathar, set about his task in an arrogant and brutal way; in May, 1239, in Champagne, he sent 187 heretics to the stake. In the south, Peter Seila and William Arnaud delivered harsh sentences and did not hesitate to have the corpses of heretics exhumed so that they could be burnt. Such severity was provocative; some prisoners were set free as a result of rioting, and the barons, who were assured of the sympathy of their subjects, tried to call in question the division of wealth and the political organization that the crusade had enforced; in May, 1242, William Arnaud and his companions were murdered on the road from Toulouse to Castelnaudary.

The effect was twofold: the king's forces laid siege to the mountain fastness of Montségur, where the Cathars took refuge whenever they were too hard pressed and where they concentrated their resources; when the fortress fell the two hundred Perfect who, led by the bishop, Bertrand Marty, refused to abandon their beliefs, were herded into an enclosure, which was set on fire. But on the other hand the Church reorganized the inquisition. The pope had already ordered an inquiry into the activities of Robert le Bougre and tried to provide a Friar Minor as assistant to each Dominican inquisitor; now councils, presided over by his legates, set about defining in precise terms the procedure to be followed so as to eliminate the element of arbitrariness.

These statutes, as well as the manuals drawn up for the use of judges, allow us to obtain a clear view of the functioning of the inquisition. It was permitted to intervene on the mere suspicion of guilt—a long-standing feature of the civil law as well; but the accused was not allowed to know the names of the witnesses, to be represented by a lawyer or to clear himself by an oath of purgation; the inquisitor, whose mission was to eradicate heresy and obtain the conversion of its exponents, bent every effort to extracting a confession, if need be by torture, the use of which was regulated by the papacy in 1252.

The seriousness of heresy in an organized religious society, whose unifying principle resided in its faith, explains the ceremony with which the judges deliberately surrounded themselves: the assembly of the populace at the moment of their arrival and before their departure; the proclamation by the crowd of the true dogma (the act of faith, the famous *auto da fé* at the moment when the sentences were read out; or the oath to reject all forms of heresy and to denounce heretics and their accomplices, which was exacted by the bishops from all the faithful who had passed the age of puberty. But although it was necessary to sustain the faith and vigilance of Christians, the ultimate object remained the return to the fold of the straying sheep. A period of grace was granted before the opening of the trial; during this period, if the accused acknowledged his error he was immediately reconciled, incurring fasting, penance and a fine. It was the contumacious, or the prisoner who had confessed only out of fear when confronted with death, who ran the risk of imprisonment—which, however harsh its conditions, never bore any relation to the hideous punishment of being walled up alive. In 1245-6, life imprisonment was ordered for one heretic in nine in the Lavaur-Castelnaudary area. Death at the stake, which could only be inflicted by the "secular arm" once the condemned person had been abandoned to it by the Church, was reserved for the relapsed, or alternatively, the accused who refused to make any confession in spite of overwhelming proof of guilt, or yet again for the person who, having confessed, refused conversion. It has been established that at Pamiers the death penalty was pronounced in one out of thirteen cases, at Toulouse in one out of twenty-three. The Count of Toulouse kept for himself the goods of those who were condemned to imprisonment or burning, but it has been proved that after satisfying the claims of families and creditors and paying expenses, he derived little more than 800 *livres tournois* a year from this source—no more than a sixth of what he received in tolls from Marmande on the Garonne.

The close collaboration of Church and princes, and the zeal that was, in general, brought to bear by the latter in repressing a spiritual aberration, cannot be understood save by the existence of the totalitarian community that was Christendom.

CHAPTER II

THE WORKS OF FAITH

Faith was the source of every activity in Christendom, and it blossomed out into works that assumed changing aspects. We have sketched the picture of a Romanesque civilization that was full of initiative, abounding in vitality, revolutionary. By comparison, the civilization of the thirteenth century, or—if one may borrow a term from art—"Gothic civilization", seems more orderly, more imposing thanks to its didactic "Mirrors" (*specula*), its encyclopedic *Summae* and its cathedrals; more realistic, and more distrustful too, with its inquisition; it had its upsurges of monastic, missionary and artistic activity, but to the very extent that its framework was more rigid, it did not manage to contain all the movements of inquiry and discovery. It had difficulty in coming to terms with the developments in wealth, pleasures and luxury that made the earth a more attractive place. It permitted the emancipation of certain elements and of a secular spirit, in spite of the fact that, in appearance, religion was stamping everything with its powerful impress.

RELIGIOUS THOUGHT AND PRACTICE

The Church's ceremonies set the rhythm by which individual and social life were lived: baptism, marriage and burial were the main stages in man's earthly itinerary; the increasingly widespread use of books of Hours, reflecting increasing literacy, allowed each moment of the day to be hallowed by the recitation of appropriate prayers; the seasons were inaugurated by Ember-day fasting; dates were reckoned by reference to the feast days of the principal saints, of which there were so many, apart from Sundays, that it became necessary to determine which ones should be marked by abstention from work and which not. Pilgrimages were still held in high regard. Even though he might show a greater fondness for social gatherings, or greater susceptibility for the poetry that celebrated love outside the ties of marriage, the knight still promised, when he received his arms, to serve rightly the cause of justice; and one of the most famous sculptures of Rheims shows a knight, armed for battle, receiving Holy Communion. The Church might disapprove of certain professions, and might maintain, somewhat ineffectually, its legislation against "usury" (to which, in fact, it gave precise definition, and in which it condemned essentially the element of profit without risk or effort); the patricians of Flanders and Italy might be impelled by love of money to exploit without pity the work of those they employed—even so, the professional associations that grew in number over the century were a reminder that their members should be united in Christian charity; they also established, with the same exactitude as for the processes of manufacture, the ceremony for celebrating the feast of their patron saint, the number of candles to be burnt, as well as the rates of contribution to their benevolent fund. Alongside the guild, which was concerned with publishing regulations about the technique and administration of the craft, the confraternity tended to occupy itself with works of charity.

A practical man, observant and interested in tangible things, the Christian of the thirteenth century found in the humanity of Jesus Christ and the discovery of the Marian graces satisfaction for his instincts of devotion. The reason for the popularity of the apocryphal gospels at that time lay in the fact that they gave information about the childhood of our Saviour and the life of his Mother. To every element of mysticism suggested by St Bernard, Franciscan influence added a note of familiarity, bringing the Gospel, the imitation of Christ, the celebration of divine glory within reach of all; it popularized the sermon, studded as it was with examples, frequently truculent,

attracting the masses and convulsing them with emotion—
with fear on the occasions when death was evoked; it encouraged the making of cribs, the first of which had been the
work of St Francis; it brought back a simple-minded vision of
nature, of a marvellous universe of brotherhood where water
and fire had souls, and man discoursed with the animals; it
prepared the way for art to represent things as they are and
not for what they signify. The general chapter of the Friars
Minor in 1263 established a feast to celebrate the Immaculate
Conception of the Blessed Virgin. Christianity, after the shock
of the First Crusade, and without losing its dramatic character
as the religion of sinful man, took on a tincture of human
warmth and borrowed the light of consolation that radiated
from the Virgin of the cathedrals.

It was about the middle of the twelfth century that the number of sacraments was fixed at seven and that they were defined
exhaustively. Not without argument, marriage was included in
the list. Though the state of virginity was still pre-eminent,
marriage, resting as it did essentially on the consent of the
partners, was conceded to be capable of leading to a high
degree of perfection. James of Vitry considered that married
people are members of an "order". The Lateran Council of
1215 enjoined annual confession and communion, at Easter,
but many confessors and synods recommended more frequent
communion. While communion of the faithful from the chalice
was decreasingly practised, devotion to the consecrated Host
provoked the introduction of new rites: people wanted to see
the Host. The Bishop of Paris, Eudes of Sully († 1208), ordered
the celebrant to raise it at arm's length, as soon as the words
of consecration had been pronounced, so that the faithful might
adore it. In 1246 at Liège, after a nun had been favoured with
visions, a feast of the Blessed Sacrament was organized; in
1263, Urban IV, on learning that a Host, at Bolsena, had been
found to be stained with blood after a clerk had expressed
doubts as to whether it was truly the Body of Christ, instituted
the triumphal procession of the *Corpus Domini*, our present

Corpus Christi; the cathedral of Orvieto was built to serve as a reliquary to house this miraculous bread. It is impossible that the intelligence of men should not have been preoccupied with the content of the faith, when their feelings were so intimately imbued with it.

THE UNIVERSITIES

A great intellectual problem arose: translations from Arabic or Hebrew, and later from Greek, were bringing to light a "new Aristotle"; in place of the fragments that until then had revealed a master of logic, it was becoming apparent that an encyclopedia of human knowledge, comprising physics, ethics and metaphysics, had been conceived without reference to divine revelation. Was there then a region in which the human mind could move without constraint? And what was its relation to the domain of faith? Was it possible to reconcile them? For the papacy, in its concern for the cohesion of Roman Christendom, it would have been a serious risk to leave the resolution of such questions to the audacious speculations of the many schools of the twelfth century. Two opportunities of supervision fortunately occurred. In the first half of the thirteenth century, both to protect themselves from the untimely intervention of the bishops or the civil authorities, and in order to organize their studies, teachers and students were adopting the habit of grouping themselves into guilds or "universities" —after the manner of the burgesses of a single town or the members of a single craft; they had a similar preoccupation with being masters in their own house. At Paris, Oxford and Montpellier, where they encouraged recognition of the grouping of the schools; at Palencia, where they supported the efforts of the King of Castile; at Toulouse, Rome, Siena and Piacenza, where they themselves instigated associations of this sort—in all these places, the popes took to themselves, in return for the privileges they granted, a right of supervision over the teaching, especially the teaching in the Faculties of Arts (through which all students passed) and of Theology: two faculties of particular importance in the formation of young minds. It was a less serious matter to countenance the emancipation of the universities of Bologna, Padua, Modena, Vicenza or Naples, which specialized in the study of civil law. On the other hand, the Holy See had at its disposal, in the ranks of the Friars Preachers and the Friars Minor, intellectual leaders whose devotion to its projects was unconditional; it could view their entry into the universities with nothing but sympathy. Once the Dominicans had come by two chairs of theology at Paris and the Franciscans one, out of a total of twelve in this discipline, the papacy took steps to see that they kept them, and was prepared to chance a mutiny among the secular teachers—as occurred between 1252 and 1257. At Oxford, it was Robert Grosseteste himself, the chancellor of the university and a professor before becoming Bishop of Lincoln, who contrived the entry of the Franciscans.

The popes and the synods had at first thought it possible to dodge the questions forced on Christian thinkers by the reading of Aristotle's work, by forbidding the teaching and discussion of the more embarrassing books. But the teachers consulted these works, they drew their inspiration from them: the prohibition was unworkable. It was better to tackle the problem boldly. The papacy gave the mendicant Orders a free hand, and they adopted two completely different attitudes.

The Franciscans, who had accepted scholarship as a necessity, could not but remember that the basis of their founder's spiritual life had consisted in the praise of God through his creation. Following St Augustine, whose thought had up till now given the intellectual tradition of Christianity its direction, they considered that reason was a subordinate instrument, limited in its applications, and that the efforts man makes to reach ultimate truth must be crowned by contemplation. Master Alexander of Hales, who adopted their grey habit about the year 1231, retained from the works of Aristotle all that might contribute to the knowledge of the sensory world, but insisted unequivocally that beyond that, the human mind had nothing further to expect save from its adherence to the truths of faith. His Italian pupil, St Bonaventure, who taught at Paris before assuming the direction of his Order, repeated that philosophical speculation had its source solely in faith, and that philosophy was justified only to the extent that it sought to establish in the sensible world the traces of God: it represented but the primary stage, the intellectual stage, of an ascension towards God, whose final stage was a mystical one.

The Dominicans did not think that the problem raised by the encyclopedic work of Aristotle could be resolved by a mere technique of filtration and the repeated assertion that reason was the handmaiden of faith. Truth, they argued, is one. There exist two means of arriving at it: either by making use of reason, so as to understand all that is demonstrable in revelation, and notably to extract from the external world proofs of the existence of God—this is the field open to philosophy; or alternatively, by following the teachings of faith, that is by accepting dogmas which are supernatural in their origin—and that is the domain of theology. But these two radically distinct approaches necessarily lead to agreement, to mutual confirmation. The German Albert of Bollstädt, honoured by the Church as St Albert the Great, undertook to expound the work of Aristotle, but did not hesitate to express his doubts, make corrections and fill in gaps; he demonstrated that the field which nature offers reason is so wide as to make it unnecessary for reason to be compromised by stepping outside the limits of nature. His disciple, Thomas Aquinas, who listened to him at Paris and Cologne, expended his genius on reconciling a science that was thoroughly human with Holy Writ. It is indeed astonishing to think that a man who lived no more than fifty years (1224–74) was able to bring off such a conspicuous undertaking, against all the odds, in his *Commentaries*, his *Quaestiones Disputatae* and his two greatest works, his *Summa contra Gentiles*, which was designed to lead unbelievers on from the observation of reality to belief in the truths of Christianity, and the *Summa Theologica*, a manual intended for the schools, in which the dialectic of scholasticism provides a means of reaching solid conclusions.

In the heat of the disputes it aroused, its contemporaries did not immediately appreciate in the Thomist synthesis the strength and mighty proportions of the reply it contained to men's questioning. But in the perspective of time, it has come to be reckoned worthy to take its place among the major successes of a Christendom that always sought to embrace, around the notion of Christianity, every human activity.

THE GOTHIC CATHEDRALS

Because it continues to stand before our eyes after six or seven centuries, familiar and yet a source of wonder, and because we piously restore it as soon as it suffers damage from the elements or the ravages of war, the Gothic cathedral is the most complete witness we have to the Christian civilization of the Middle Ages—is, indeed, a symbol of the West as a whole. It would be difficult to find anyone today who used the adjective "Gothic" with the nuance of barbarity and scorn that its coiners intended; but it would be no less mistaken to surround it with the mirages of the romantic imagination. The building and its style express quite definite social, historical and religious realities. They are not evocative of the forests of Gaul and Germany, as was thought by Goethe and Chateaubriand when they stood in the half-light contemplating the alignment of columns; and Victor Hugo was no less wide of the mark when, obsessed by his vision of a world of forms in conflict, tender or monstrous, he saw them as manifesting the emancipation of the communes, the impassioned protest of thinkers struggling against the coalition of spiritual and social oppression. They are neither the catalogue of symbols that the novelist Huysmans read in them, nor the mere impeccable solution of successive geometrical problems that they become in the works of the French architect and antiquarian Viollet-le-Duc.

The "Gothic manner" emerged by degrees, during the first two thirds of the twelfth century, from the various points of Romanesque experimentation in Normandy, Poitou and the Ile-de-France, and in the abbeys of the Cistercian order. It benefited from the exploration that had been made of the possibilities offered by the pointed arch, and even more by rib vaulting which allowed for a higher covering to the nave and a more precise localization of the lines of thrust. It corresponded to a religious feeling based on repose and contemplation of God's goodness, of the humanity of Jesus and of the touching figure of the Blessed Virgin Mary, rather than on prostration before the awful power of the Supreme Judge returning in triumph at the end of time. It underwent the influence of an age which, breaking free of the imaginary world, enumerated the various aspects of creation, learnt to regard them as they were, and faithful to the notion that things visible are but the reflection of supernatural realities, drew up the inventory of human knowledge in as many "mirrors" or compendia as was necessary to understand Nature, Science, Morality and History, as in the work of Vincent of Beauvais. Lastly, the growth of the towns and the increase in wealth stimulated the demands, the capital and the commissions without which it is impossible for art to flourish. The "building mania" of which Peter the Troubadour speaks at the end of the twelfth century testifies to the confident assurance with which the West set about doing homage to God.

To order all the elements that concur to determine a style, to conceive the great cathedrals, it was necessary to have a master craftsman of genius. The master craftsmen of the thirteenth century were conscious of their worth and did not remain anonymous. Villard of Honnecourt's book of plans and sketches has come down to us from this age. It was with these great masters, and with the specialist teams of masons, sculptors and glassmakers, with a whole host of artisans, that the bishops and the chapters dealt; generally, they appointed an administrator to take charge of the undertaking, since the necessary funds had to be raised and managed, and this financial responsibility was a heavy one—how many churches were never finished, or were so long in building that the original plan was unrecognizable! It is imperative to dispel the naïve illusion by which this painstaking labour is seen as the enthusiastic work of amateurs hauling wagonloads of stone and swarming on to the scaffolding. The cooperative work of the faithful was al-together exceptional at Chartres, where following a fire in 1194, in their devotion to Notre-Dame-sous-Terre, all worked together; what was principally asked of Christian citizens was their money.

The Gothic building obeys a complex and powerful harmony, the responsibility for which is borne by the architecture, which does not merely distribute volumes and assign to the other disciplines the areas within which they are to be deployed, as in the Romanesque conception; it imposes its style on the details no less than on the whole. It is fond of vertical lines, it sends pillars, towers, bell-turrets and pinnacles soaring upwards, and carries the point of its arches to a hundred, a hundred and twenty feet, and more. It provides a framework so solid and at the same time so light that, once sure of its means, it tends to transform the church into a glass cage, as in the upper storey of the Sainte-Chapelle in Paris. It establishes the ornamental rôle to be played by sculpture, stained glass, painting and tapestry; the sculptors worked on the building site, cutting the stones whose decoration had been entrusted to them and which, as soon as they were ready, were put in position by the masons. It is because sculpture was an integral part of the architectural unit that the Huguenots and the Revolutionaries were able to do no more than knock off projections and dislodge heads; to have effaced the Gothic impression they would have had to demolish completely. All the arts were subordinated to the intentions of the master craftsman, obeyed the same architectural rhythm; the same forms are found in wall paintings and stained glass windows, in furniture and jewellery, in miniatures and ivories, and even in the script of the time, with its slender, angular lines.

The whole humanity of an age breathes in the Gothic cathedral. It is not peopled by visions sprung from remotest ages like its Romanesque predecessor, but by harmonious figures, where a smile lights up the face, and serenity is offset by a slight contortion. Alternatively, it may simply welcome peasants and craftsmen at work. The decoration shows an accurate observation of people, animals and vegetation and, where exact reproduction is wanting, a sense of the lifelike and the moderate. Its symbolism is simple; every Christian with the slightest pretension to culture knew that the heroes and scenes of the Old Testament prefigured those of the New. In any case, the subjects were living and beautiful in themselves; even when they betrayed the hand of less skilled workmen they bore witness to a civilization that regarded it as the completely natural thing to offer to God all it knew and did. Jacques Maritain has written: "The builders of cathedrals were not intending to demonstrate the relevance of Christian dogma, nor to use artifice to suggest a Christian emotion. . . . They believed, and as they were, they built. Their work revealed the truth of God, but it was not their aim—or rather, because it was not their aim."

It is not my intention to trace the development of this art in time and space, or its variations; except in Italy, it called into being the world of forms in which, for some three centuries, the inspiration of the West expressed itself; in almost every part of the world to which Roman Christendom penetrated, from the shores of the Baltic to the Iberian peninsula and the coasts of Syria won by the crusaders, it carried its proof of the faith.

THE BEGINNINGS OF EMANCIPATION

From the middle of the thirteenth century, however, the unity of the Gothic style began to break up. The various arts which had been strictly subordinated to architecture tended to shake themselves free, to live their own life. Lay commissions began to come in for large town houses, for law courts and guild halls; people began to look on art as an embellishment to life. And they began asking it to reproduce their features: the age of the portrait was at hand.

At the very moment when it was effected, the reconciliation of philosophical inquiry with the teachings of revealed religion was called in question. In the Faculty of Arts of the University of Paris, teachers were interpreting Aristotle with the help of the commentaries of the Arab Averroes; they denied that it was possible to establish a concordance between the thought of the Peripatetics and the Christian faith; they therefore accepted that there were two truths, and on that pretext followed the philosopher who affirmed the eternity of the world and the existence of a single Intelligence. How could the Church tolerate such an intellectual attitude, in spite of the homage paid to the teachings of faith by such as Siger of Brabant and Boethius of Dacia? The Dominican doctors abounded in refutations; the Bishop of Paris pronounced a first condemnation in 1270, but as the "Latin Averroists" did not acknowledge themselves beaten, he found it advisable, as the Archbishop of Canterbury had done, to forbid any propositions to be drawn from Aristotle: in 1277, in a list of 219 propositions condemned by the authorities of the Church, were to be found not only the opinions of Siger of Brabant and his group, but several articles accepted by St Thomas Aquinas. Whatever may have been the immediate effect of the condemnation, a new idea of the philosopher's rôle had emerged from these bitter disputes—that of an upright and virtuous intelligence, divorced from pleasures, putting its trust in mental techniques and human powers, involved in the world, finding God, no doubt, at the end of its path, but through observing creation and no longer taking flight toward him on the wings of a mystical impulse. This has been called a typically secular spirituality.

In literature, an ideal wholly based on naturalism ventured to raise its standard. The epic and courtly forms were enmeshed in symbolism; the urban audiences preferred the animal romance, the irreverent *fabliau*, the satire and plays satirizing manners, berating the clergy, waxing ironical at the expense of knightly customs, and rich in coarse pleasantries. But the bantering wit of these authors—Adam de la Halle, Rutebeuf, those who devised the story of Reynard the Fox—however it may have prepared the way for the spirit of free judgement, did no damage to anything essential. Quite different was the case of Jean de Meung who, about 1275, added a continuation of eighteen thousand lines to Guillaume de Lorris's *Romance of the Rose*; he did not fear to question the whole moral, social and political order. Doubtless the wandering clerks of the previous century, the Goliards, in their state of perpetual revolt had spoken the same language; but theirs had been a lost cause from the start. Jean de Meung's enormous and laboured poetic output expressed a much more formidable and wide-ranging anger and cynicism. Neither courtly love, marriage, chivalry, property, government nor the clergy found grace in his eyes; he exalted nature, railed at chastity; he trusted in the fecundity of the species, and denounced the established powers for their brutal use of force and their ability to exploit the weak; in his work, the Lover picked the Rose. Jean de Meung did not deny God, but left him to the theologians. It was in Nature that he invited man to take his pleasure.

In a completely contrasted spirit, the Franciscans of Britain at the same time were directing the attention of the intelligence towards observable facts. Following in the footsteps of his patron, Robert Grosseteste, Roger Bacon at Oxford was urging the drawing up of a scientific inventory of the universe, in preference to a description of it after the Aristotelian manner. In his *Opus Maior*, of about 1266, he stressed an intellectual procedure at complete variance with that of the teachers at Paris: he insisted on the necessity of acquiring a solid philological and mathematical culture before undertaking the study of the natural sciences, and he demanded that all deductions should be verified by experiment. But his lack of prudence brought about his condemnation in the very year when St Thomas's work was disavowed by the ecclesiastical authorities. Bacon's work was forgotten, but the new tradition he had exemplified did not disappear.

Thus, in art, literature and philosophy, the effort at homogeneity that the Holy See was also pursuing in political practice and theory was breached. The major syntheses, which constituted the successes of a Christendom deeply involved in the world and trying to discipline it, were disputed. Two paths were beginning to appear, on which those minds who renounced agreement and unity were resolutely setting out. In the first place there was the temptation of individualism: the layman, with his increased store of intellectual riches, who thrashed out civic matters, whether in his town or at the centre of his village community, who handled money and calculated his profit, was quite happy to do without the clergy, whom he looked on with irony, if not distrust; he was encouraged in this attitude by the disagreement between the secular clergy and the mendicant Orders; on one side he put everything over which he had control—his business, if he was a merchant; his teaching and speculation, if he was an intellectual—and on the other he put religion. For he was devout, beginning his account books by invoking the Trinity and the Blessed Virgin, keeping aside, in the accounts of commercial enterprises, a portion for the poor, founding chapels, leaving his goods to works of charity. But this man, who split his life into two parts, who for preference gave his attention to worldly matters, was surely breaking a harmony, preparing the fragmentation of a civilization whose cohesion he was disregarding?

Another way out presented itself to those who were dissatisfied with the positions taken up by the pope, the clergy and the monks, felt to be too compromised in politics and wealth. They might give themselves up to a mystical exaltation and wait to see the triumph of religion, in spirit and in truth, come about in apocalyptic upheavals. The Calabrian Joachim, Abbot of Flora, who had died at the very opening of the thirteenth century, had announced the imminent advent of a new age, that of the Holy Spirit (the period of the Old Testament being the age of the Father, the New Testament that of the Son); his successors had developed his vision—the visible Church was condemned to disappear and the "eternal Gospel", whose meaning lay hidden in the New Testament, would inspire the final phase of man's spiritual adventure. Within the Franciscan Order, the "Spirituals", who took zeal for the most complete form of poverty to be the touchstone of loyalty to their founder's spirit, and who rejected all the compromises decreed by the Holy See, saw themselves as the heralds of the new age. There were Christians who, without following their heretical example, were attracted into the paths of this mystical love, and grew increasingly indifferent to the world of contingents. But this too was an escape, another way of allowing things temporal to follow their own course; that is, of giving up the attempt to reconcile them with the demands of the spiritual.

CHAPTER III

THEOCRACY AND ITS LIMITATIONS

Not only did the Church hold a privileged position that allowed her to extend her influence over a wide area of social and intellectual life, but over and above this she strove to dominate political organization and trends. It was this ambitiousness in temporal matters that constitutes the originality of medieval Christendom.

THE CLAIMS OF THEOCRACY

Theocratic doctrine ascribed to the pope, as head of the Church, an overriding authority in the affairs of the world. We have already seen this authority exercised on frequent occasions; we have heard Gregory VII, Urban II, Alexander III and Innocent III justify it. Never, though, was the claim so clearly made and explained as in the middle of the thirteenth century.

Gregory IX (1227–41) took up again the historical argument based on the Donation of Constantine, namely, that the emperor had not made a transfer of his authority to the papacy, but had merely restored a power that he had been wielding illegitimately. The Empire was a dependency of the Holy See, not accidentally but in essence. Innocent IV (1243–54), great jurist that he was, expressed the theocratic conception in all its fullness and logic; the Bull *Eger cui levia* of 1245 can be regarded as its clearest manifesto:

> Whoever seeks to evade the authority of the Vicar of Christ . . .
> thereby impairs the authority of Christ himself. The King of

Kings has established us on earth as his universal representative and has conferred full power on us by giving to the Prince of the Apostles and to us the power of binding and loosing on earth not only all men whatsoever, but also all things whatsoever.... The Roman Pontiff may exercise his pontifical power over every Christian at least as an occasional right..., *a fortiori* by reason of sin. The power of temporal government cannot be exercised outside the Church, since there is no power constituted by God outside her.... They are lacking in perspicacity and incapable of investigating the origin of things, who imagine that the Apostolic See received from Constantine the sovereignty of the Empire, whereas it had it previously, as is known, by nature and potentially. Our Lord Jesus Christ, Son of God, true man and true God, true king and true priest according to the order of Melchisedech..., constituted to the benefit of the Holy See a monarchy not only pontifical but royal; he committed to the Blessed Peter and his successors the reins of the empire both earthly and celestial, as is indicated by the plurality of the keys. Vicar of Christ, [the pope] has received the power to exercise his jurisdiction by the one over the earth for temporal things, by the other in heaven for spiritual things.

The canonists, Henry of Susa and William Durandus the Elder, took up these arguments in order to demonstrate clearly that the emperor—*a fortiori* any other prince—was only the lieutenant of the Roman pontiff, who was empowered to judge everything as it pleased him. In a powerful vision of the historical destiny of mankind, Roger Bacon, in his *Opus Tertium*, imagined the pope, guardian of Scripture and, by the same token, master of Wisdom, as bringing together under his authority the Church and "the republic of the faithful" which, for her part, was destined progressively to embrace the universe.

These assertions were not mere gratuitous speculation; men had fought for them, they corresponded to conflicting ambitions; they were at once weapons of war and commentaries on it. Innocent III's former ward, Frederick II, piling on his head the crowns of Sicily, Germany, Jerusalem and the Empire, had

accused the pope of abusing his power when he dared to dis-
possess him of his temporal sword; for him, the competences
and functions were distinct; the Church was sovereign in spiritual matters, the State in temporal. Constantine had not been
legitimately empowered to part with his possessions irrevocably, he had not committed his successors. The Empire
corresponded to a necessity of nature and a design of Provi-
dence; it was entrusted with seeing that Justice reigned on
earth, and its seat was at Rome; it was no part of its duties
to subjugate the kingdoms, which in their turn proceeded from
God, but to associate them with it in a secular body, which
should safeguard the independence of the princes against the
threats of the papacy, and protect the Christian commonwealth
from the ravages of heresy. In such a view, Christendom would
still have existed, but its form would have been very different
from that which the Roman Church had for two centuries been
striving to give it.

These arguments Frederick II, who showed very little personal regard for Christian law, borrowed partly from a hetero-
geneous but exceptionally rich heritage, and partly from his
Sicilian cultural background, in which Latin, Greek, Arabic
and Jewish influences were all merged. The importance he
actually attached to them is a matter of discussion among his-
torians. In any event, even when he called on the kings to rise
up against pontifical omnipotence, he found no response. His
ambition and his pride, which were served by an uncommon
political genius, consisted above all in enjoying complete
sovereignty within his own state; and the latter, in the tradition
of his family, he could only conceive as uniting Italy and
Germany; to succeed in this, he had to isolate the Holy See
within a limited function and deprive it of any means of intervening in the affairs of the peninsula. In the grandeur of two
claims to universality, meeting head on, there was fought out an
implacable duel in which Italy was the prize: a fact which
considerably reduced the dimensions of the struggle.

THE DEFEAT OF THE EMPIRE AND WHAT IT MEANT

Owing to the fact that his son was still a child, Frederick retained the government of Sicily and that of Germany. By announcing his imminent departure for the crusade, he put the Holy See in an indulgent mood. Honorius III granted him coronation as emperor in 1220. But Gregory IX was not to be hoodwinked in this manner; on November 18th, 1227, he excommunicated the emperor. Frederick left Italy without receiving absolution; while he was having himself recognized King of Jerusalem (having married the heiress to that throne) and persuading the Sultan of Egypt to restore the Holy City in return for allowing Mohammedans freedom to worship in two mosques, the pope released his Sicilian subjects from their oath of loyalty and sent an army to conquer the fief of the disloyal vassal. Finally, in 1230, a reconciliation was achieved, in return for concessions to the Holy See over the administration of the Church in Sicily.

Frederick II renewed his authoritarian policy in Italy and Germany; after crushing the towns of Lombardy, he announced his intention of installing himself at Rome and choosing the proconsuls of the provinces from among the nobility of the city. The days of the papacy's temporal freedom seemed numbered: putting forward religious grievances as a counter to the emperor's ecclesiastical policy, Gregory IX excommunicated him for a second time, in 1239.

The temporal fate of Italy, the future of the Papal States, was in the balance. It was at this stage that, in their manifestos, the adversaries debated the problem of the relation between the two powers in the government of the world.

They were not sparing in their use of invective: "monster [who] opens his mouth only to calumniate the name of God", "precursor of Antichrist", wrote the pope of Frederick; "Pharisee, seated on a throne of pestilence . . . , a man who has but the name of a pope, a great dragon who is only Antichrist himself" retorted the emperor. Frederick occupied the march of Ancona and the duchy of Spoleto, in the Papal States, but Gregory roused the towns of Lombardy and convened a council. At the emperor's instigation, the Pisan fleet intercepted the Genoese ships that were carrying the prelates. Gregory seemed likely to be besieged in Rome when he died in 1241.

Innocent IV extricated himself skilfully from this critical situation; he established himself in his native city of Genoa, and then at Lyons, on the frontier of the French kingdom on whose support he could count in the event of danger. Time was on his side: the German ecclesiastical princes revolted against the emperor, the great towns of northern Italy held firm, the mendicants preached against the excommunicated emperor. At Lyons, Innocent IV was able to call a general council; despite the efforts of the imperial advocate, Frederick was condemned: on July 17th, 1245, he was deprived of "all his honours and dignities", deposed, and excommunicated for a third time. The pontiff showed great tenacity in carrying out the sentence; through his legates and through the monks, he brought about the election of a new king in Germany, he called on the cities of Italy to revolt, and he promised to those who fought the rebel the same indulgences as to the crusaders. Supported as he was by the lay princes, master of vast areas in central Italy, and based on the kingdom of Sicily, Frederick might perhaps have held the pope in check if he had not met his death in 1250.

The union of Germany and Italy was irrevocably compromised. For more than twenty years Germany was plunged into the disorders of "the great interregnum"; the elected kings who quarrelled over the shadow of power were foreigners, Alfonso X of Castile and the King of England's brother, Richard, Earl of Cornwall; when Gregory X, distressed at this weakness of Christian Germany at a time when he desired to launch another great crusading project, strove for the restoration of kingly authority, the electors, in preference to the wealthy King of Bohemia, chose the Landgrave of Alsace, Rudolph of Hapsburg, in 1273. Rudolph promised to take the cross and to come and receive the imperial crown, but he crossed neither the sea nor the Alps; what engaged his attention was the recovery of the lands and rights lost by his predecessors.

Italy had to withstand the successive onslaughts of one of Frederick's sons, Conrad IV, one of his bastards, Manfred, and finally his grandson, Conradin. The successes they won showed how precarious was the pope's authority in a land rent asunder, where the Guelphs, supporters of the papacy, opposed the Ghibellines who were friendly to the Empire, where the cities were given over to implacable rivalries, and where the Romans were seeking to restore the sovereignty of their city. Popes of French nationality saw their only hope of salvation in an appeal to a branch of the Capetian tree: Charles, Count of Anjou and Provence, was invested with the kingdom of Sicily; he was given a tithe on the revenues of the Church of France and his expedition was accorded the status of a crusade. In 1268, he was victorious. He, now, was the master of Italy; a three-year vacancy in the see of Rome favoured his plans. He had at his disposal the best organized state in the peninsula, he had himself named senator of Rome and vicar of Tuscany; he sent agents to the north. He mapped out a grand Mediterranean policy: it was a dream that crumbled in the revolt of 1282 in Palermo, known as the Sicilian Vespers, in the seizure of Sicily by the Aragonese and in the King of France's pointless campaign of revenge in Aragon. But the papacy was now no more than one of the powers in an Italy more divided than ever; it had difficulty in winning respect for itself even within the frontiers of its own territory.

Such a reduction of political action to the scale of Italian affairs threw the grand ideas of universal power back into the realm of Utopia: there was no point of extolling the Germanic Empire during the afflictions of the long interregnum, of propounding the idea that the imperial office was at the service of the Roman people when the latter registered so little emotion at the invitations and blandishments of Manfred and Conradin, of subscribing to the sacerdotal theory that the Holy See should dispose of the Empire and assume the administration of Italy during a vacancy, when the forces of dismemberment were triumphant.

There had always been a certain lack of correlation between the struggles as they actually took place and the ideological interpretation given to them; after the middle of the thirteenth century, the dissociation became so obvious that the conceptions of both papacy and Empire lost all contact with reality and corresponded to nothing more than the speculations of intellectuals or dreamers. The problem of the political form of Christendom, to which the answers, since Carolingian times, and with more or less of success, had always taken a unitary form, was now, in point of fact, beyond the reach of the two traditional contenders. The effect of the Italian dispute was reinforced by the rebuffs to the papacy in the East and the rise of the western monarchies.

FAILURE IN THE EAST

From the eleventh century two preoccupations had loomed largest in papal thinking, namely the submission of the schismatic Greek Church to its tutelage and the maintenance of the positions acquired in Syria by the crusade. The establishment of a Latin empire at Constantinople had opened up unforeseen possibilities for it. By the end of the thirteenth century, all its hopes were dashed.

In 1261, Michael VII Palaeologus retook Constantinople; of the western conquests of 1204 there remained only a few principalities in central and southern Greece, and some islands under the control of Venice, threatened in both cases. The papacy had been unable clearly to make up its mind: until 1240 or so, it had upheld the Latin emperor and had not shrunk from taking the initiative in veritable crusading expeditions against the Greeks of Nicaea. Innocent IV had realized that the Latin domination was doomed and that no religious reconciliation would take place as long as Constantinople was occupied by the successors of the crusaders. He went a long way in discussions to win the obedience of the eastern clergy, but the fair words he felt obliged to address to the Latin emperor thwarted his policy. It was impossible to achieve anything until the Greeks returned in force to their capital.

But then the Emperor Michael made a fresh approach. The conditions surrounding the long negotiations explain their lack of success, and the precariousness of such conclusions as were reached. The emperor feared a counter-offensive from the Latins, and later the intriguing of Charles of Anjou; the majority of the clergy—and particularly the monks—and the mass of the population, who were attached to their own rites and exasperated by half a century of Frankish domination, would not hear of submission to Rome. The pope was undecided between the temptation to help in reconstituting a Latin empire in the East and the desire to gather all the Churches under his spiritual authority; he even had the momentary vision of a new crusade undertaken by the forces of a reunited Christendom. The sacerdotal zeal of Gregory X and the eagerness of Michael VII to ward off the threat represented by Charles of Anjou did, however, lead to the union of 1274; at the Council of Lyons, the Greek ambassadors, among whom figured a few prelates, recognized the primacy of the Roman Church and subscribed to its symbol of faith, which was solemnly sung in Latin and Greek. It was an equivocal agreement, and the cause of the reconciliation was unpopular at Byzantium. The proclamation of the union by a Greek council in 1277 was hedged about with reservations. Finally, in 1281, Michael was declared to be guilty of fomenting heresy and schism, and was excommunicated. Charles set about preparing a campaign against him that had all the appearances of a crusade.

The cupidity aroused by the possession of Constantinople was one of the causes of the loss of the Frankish colonies in Syria. Since there were now only a small number of people animated by a mystical urge towards the Holy Places, and since the mutual distrust of the papacy and the monarchies made it impossible for them to initiate any more great movements of popular enthusiasm, the least that would have been necessary would have been a vigorous military effort to preserve the conquests of the first barons. No coherent overall movement could be organized, despite the meticulous prescriptions of the council of 1215, the ardour of Louis IX of France and the passion of Gregory X. Two serious attempts, that united diplomacy with a demonstration of strength, were without lasting results: the agreement under which Frederick II had recovered Jerusalem, Bethlehem and Nazareth was brought to nothing fifteen years later by an attack of the Sultan of Egypt's mercenaries, who seized the Holy City in 1244. The cooperation conceived by St Louis between Mongol troops coming out of the East and a Christian expedition directed on the West, did not materialize; Louis had been taken prisoner, then liberated on payment of a very heavy ransom; he had waited in vain in Outremer for four years, when the Tartars thrust as far as Aleppo and Damascus. A few years later the new rulers of Egypt undertook to liquidate the Frankish domination in Syria. Tyre, Sidon, Beirut and Acre held out until 1291.

To the West, there remained only the island outpost of Cyprus, which in any case had been wrested from the Byzantines. And it was true also that it was through the initiative of rulers—Frederick II (who happened to be under excommunication at this moment) and St Louis, King of France—that the two best chances of survival had come to the Frankish states. No better evidence could be found of the failure of papal policies and of Christendom's powerlessness to unite in order to preserve its common property.

THE TACTICS OF THE PRINCES

A policy for Christendom would again be envisaged many times after this; but it already seemed incapable of realization at the moment when papal theocrats were expressing it in the most categorical forms. Throughout the West, in the thirteenth century, the princes were acting in accordance with their own interests.

It was they who initiated, and they who profited from, the territorial gains of Christianity. In the north-east, beyond the Elbe and the Saale, in the areas around the Baltic, the Count of Holstein, the Duke of Saxony, the Margrave of Brandenburg, the Polish dukes, the King of Denmark and the King of Sweden directed a simultaneous enterprise of conquest, colonization and evangelization. When Albrecht of Bremen, after being elevated to the see of Riga, directed operations in Livonia with the help of his Knights of the Sword (*Ensiferi*), his intention was to carve himself out a principality on the lines of the very powerful ones that already existed around the episcopal towns of the Rhine. When, in 1226, the Polish Duke of Masovia called on the monk-knights of the Teutonic Order, at that time serving in the Holy Land, for help in throwing back the Prussians, he was opening the way for a merciless work of occupation and extermination, for which the Grand Master of the Order, Hermann of Salza, obtained from the emperor sovereign rights identical with those the German princes had won for themselves. The papacy was so clearly aware of the danger that it wanted to transform the knights' offensive into a crusade, as St Bernard had attempted to do less than a century earlier, and it proclaimed its rights of overlordship in the conquered Prussian territories. The practical effect was slight; the intervention of the Holy See was successful only in the organization of the new dioceses, which it put under Dominicans for preference.

The national aspect of the struggle against the unbeliever was even more strongly marked in the Iberian peninsula. The bands of crusaders who had answered Innocent III's call had almost all returned across the Pyrenees after the Christian army's victory at Las Navas de Tolosa in 1212. And to his cousin Louis IX of France, who was urging him to espouse the cause of the Holy Land, the King of Castile and León, St Ferdinand III, was in a position to reply, "There is no lack

of infidels in our country". The honour fell to him of entering
Córdoba and Seville and of opening up the road to Cadiz,
while the King of Portugal completed the occupation of the
province of Algarve and the King of Aragon, James I, seized
the Balearic Islands and Valencia. From the end of the thirteenth century, there remained to Islam only Upper Andalusia
with the Granada Basin and the coastal strips of Almeria and
Málaga. The rulers were strengthening their authority, giving
themselves over to vast political schemes: the house of Aragon
dreamed of making itself preponderant in the western Mediterranean basin, and rose in opposition to the no less ambitious
projects of Charles of Anjou, the pope's protégé. The kings
of Castile controlled the military orders of Calatrava and Al-
cántara which kept watch over their frontiers; they granted
guarantees to the Muslim groups in the reconquered cities—
the *mudéjares*—and to the Jews.

Intellectual life was no more immune than politics to
national influences. During three-quarters of the thirteenth
century, it was the France of the Capets that set the pattern:
in Germany and the Holy Land, in Spain and Italy, what the
public liked was the courtly lyric, the epic or the romance,
in the style—and even in the language—of their French origi-
nators; Gothic art spread across the western world, showing
unmistakable traces of its French origin. If, about the middle
of the century, there was a perceptible unity in artistic and
intellectual civilization, it was thanks to the hegemony of
Louis IX's kingdom. And when this prestige was lost, it was
to make way for vernacular, popular literatures, or for another
national influence centred, this time, in Italy—the Italy that
made use of an antiquity it had rediscovered to give new life
to lyricism, and above all to plastic and graphic art.

It is difficult to see how the kingdoms should have forborne
to manifest their impatience with a clergy that wanted autonomy within a national community, or with a pope who was
always intervening in Church matters. The more insistent demands and the strengthened means of action at the disposal

of the royal powers, based as they were on new conceptions of the state, were responsible for the increasing bitterness and frequency of conflicts of jurisdiction and protests against the appointment of beneficiaries and the levying of subsidies. Henry III of England gave a respectful welcome to the papal legate in 1237, but warned him against promulgating any decrees that might be contrary to the prerogatives of the English crown. In France, Louis IX despatched an embassy to Innocent IV at Lyons to point out the damage that papal practices were causing to the churches of the kingdom; and as the pope made the high-handed retort that he was resolved on maintaining the rights of the see of Rome, he was given a statement that such methods would not be tolerated, and that it was the king's intention "to reserve to himself and the needs of the kingdom the wealth [of the church establishments], which he is free to use as his own goods". Frederick II was unsuccessful in whipping the princes up against the papacy, but he was not mistaken in thinking that, if he had a chance, it lay in rousing them against the pretensions of the theocrats. It was about 1260 that the "Book of Justice and Pleas" (*Le Livre de Justice et de Plet*) posited the principle that "what pleases the prince has force of law".

THE EXAMPLE OF ST LOUIS

A new picture of the West was emerging, that of a collection of independent kingdoms, whose heads were the sole judges of their interests, accepting from the Church, and in particular from the pope, no more than the recollection of the precepts of the Gospels and the spiritual principles that a Christian society is bound to respect and defend. Ascetical treatises, in the tradition of the Byzantine works on imperial asceticism and mysticism, now emphasized, not the modes of sacerdotalism, but the rules which should inform kings in their private as in their public conduct, that they might be equal to their lofty vocation as leaders of Christian peoples.

A monk to whom frontiers were unknown, St Bernard, had embodied the ideal of Roman Christendom in the twelfth century; a hundred years later it was a king, St Louis, who set the example of what the Christendom of the princes might have been if all had acted as he did.

To appreciate him as he deserves, it is necessary both to divest him of the mantle of affected piety with which some have wrapped him, and to reject economic prosperity as sufficient explanation of his reign. It is enough to listen to his own words and the testimony of those who knew him, and compare them with the pattern of his life. At the source of all, there was a burning faith: "Fair son," he wrote to his heir, "the first thing I teach you is that you set your heart to love God; for, without that, no man can be saved. Preserve yourself from doing anything that is unpleasing to God." As a man, he was exemplary: his ambition was to be morally impeccable, to be worthy of being called a *prudhomme*, which "is so good and great a thing that even to pronounce it fills the mouth". He knew the injunction to charity; he practised it with the magnanimity of a king and the simplicity of one who was "poor in spirit". "He had charity towards his neighbour, and an orderly and virtuous compassion," testifies William of St Pathus. He would not have allowed the government of his kingdom to be ruled by other principles than those that directed his private acts. Justice tempered with charity, that was his public programme. He advised the future Philip III:

> If it happens that you become king, take care that you have the qualities befitting a king, that is, that you are so upright that you never decline from it no matter what may befall. If it happens that there is a dispute between a poor man and a rich man, uphold the poor man more than the rich man until such time as you know the truth, and when you shall know the truth, do the right. ... If it comes to your knowledge that you hold a thing wrongly, whether from your own time or from the time of your forbears, return it immediately, however great the

thing be, either in lands or coin or in other respects. [The constant concern is that] you should see to it diligently that your attendants and your subjects live under you in peace and in uprightness.

Thus Louis IX enjoyed rendering meticulous justice himself, sending officials to investigate the complaints that his agents' administration might have raised; it was on considerations of honesty that he argued for the issuing of a sound coinage. Louis agreed to restore certain territories in the south-west of the kingdom to Henry III, King of England and Duke of Aquitaine, although the latter had been duly defeated on the field of battle; when the French barons criticized Louis for this, he advanced the argument that not only had Henry done him a liegeman's homage, but especially that this was a way to put an end to an interminable conflict, by establishing "love between the children" of the two families. His moral prestige was not confined to France: from England to the Dauphiné he was sought as an arbitrator, for no unjust ambition could be discerned in him; did he not command his son "not to have, in so far as it depended on him, any war against Christians"?

On the other hand, he could conceive of no higher form of service than that of the common interest of Christendom, the crusade. If this great project had been salvable, it would have been through him; he devoted the strength of the most powerful monarchy in the West to this cause, he gave himself to it without remission for six years, from 1248 to 1254, and finally sacrificed himself to it, since he was carried off by illness on August 25th, 1270, having reached Tunis on the new expedition he was organizing. Doubtless he was deficient in realism. But his partners should have been saints like himself! How admirably what was best in the thirteenth century found its harmony in him: St Francis of Assisi's spirit of penitence, gentleness and joy (he was a member of the Third Order); the calm firmness of the leader who replied to his brother Charles of Anjou that "there should only be one king in France"; the mystic sense of the obligations of Christendom—"My faithful friends," he explained to his companions before Damietta in 1249, "we shall be invincible if we are inseparable in our charity; I am not the King of France, I am not the Holy Church, it is you, in so far as you are all king, who are the Holy Church."

PART II

DISINTEGRATION

From the eleventh century onwards, the papacy, while losing its hold over the eastern Church, had made sure of a growing influence in western Christianity; at the beginning of the fourteenth century, it was maintained in some quarters that "where the pope is, there is Rome" since it was in the person of its head that the source of authority resided, and a theologian who wanted to describe the Church would begin by defining the institution of the papacy. The successor to the apostle Peter, the Vicar of Christ had claimed for himself a right of supervision extending over the government of the world; it was under his supreme responsibility that he envisaged the temporal history of Christendom. In spite of some successes, neither the centralization of the Church—which must take into account the multiplicity and particularism of clerical organization—nor, *a fortiori*, the ambition to direct secular affairs had been fully realized. But it was only at the very end of the thirteenth century and during the course of the fourteenth that these claims encountered formal opposition. Then, while war, famine, pestilence, economic difficulties and social upheavals were destroying the material equilibrium of the West, first the conception the Church had formed of its rôle, and then the constitution it had adopted were called in question. Quite naturally, attacks were directed against the papacy, which had raised itself to an exceptional position; its battles and its reverses must necessarily occupy our attention in the first place. When it ended by being torn between the rival claims of two holders, each equally certain of his legitimacy, how was it possible for the theologians, the lawyers and the simple faithful not to ask themselves whether the Church should not be established on a new basis? This storm without a precedent reawakened old or produced new heresies, and provided the princes with an opportunity to take charge of the Churches in their domains. Along with the other crises that shook the West, it transformed feeling, shattered convictions and led to new ideas. In keeping with the disarray of the age were the passion and the uncertainties in aesthetic experiment, spiritual transports and philosophical speculation. If, around the middle of the fifteenth century, the Church appeared to be re-established, it could not regain, either in the intellectual or the political domain, the dominant position it had lost. The era of Christendom was closed for all time. It is the story of its break-up we must now retrace in outline.

CHAPTER IV

THE END OF THE DREAM
OF TEMPORAL UNITY

It was not new systems of thought that first threatened the Church's position: the voices urging a scientific exploration of the world of sense or refusing the attempt to harmonize faith and reason were the voices of unbelievers, and the Church did not profess an official philosophy. The heresies preserved among the Waldensians and Cathars had not yet been revived. It was the theory of theocracy that provoked dispute; although it had been coherently formulated, it had never won the assent of the princes it claimed to control, nor for long proved its practical efficacy; but it represented the Roman vision of Christendom and a unifying principle. Brandished with intransigence, it provoked, now, formal rejection and refutation, and its overthrow immediately reacted on the institution of the papacy which, from the middle of the eleventh century, had been ordering its western policy by referring to it.

To understand the conflict, it is not only necessary to invoke the rigour of legal reasoning and the arrogant, hot-headed temper of Boniface VIII; the curious and disturbing crisis to which the latter's election put an end on December 24th, 1294, must also be borne in mind. For the space of two years, the cardinals had been unable to agree on the name of a candidate; one of them finally drew their attention to a hermit in the Abruzzi, Peter, who was living a life devoted to pious and ascetic exercises on Monte Magella or Monte Murrone; the holy man was elected pontiff and took the name of Celestine V. Lacking experience, he fell under two influences, that of the King of

Sicily, Charles II, who installed him at Naples, and that of the so-called "Spiritual" Franciscans, who were convinced that detachment from the world was necessary and that the Holy Spirit would shortly be triumphant: they hailed in Celestine the inaugurator of a new age. Whether through subjection to a prince or loss of interest in temporal matters, the papacy was in a fair way to abandoning what had been its mission for several centuries. Celestine V was fully aware of his inadequacy; he was completely without ambition, and had no more intention of committing the Church to a new spiritual course than he had of compromising its political rôle; he abdicated after a reign of six months. He was replaced by Cardinal Benedetto Caetani, who had been his counsellor. In these circumstances, it is not surprising that Boniface VIII thought it necessary to demonstrate the full scope of the powers claimed by the Holy See; hence the return of the curia from Naples to Rome, the imprisonment of Peter di Murrone, the reaffirmation of the view that the pope had transferred the Empire to the Germans as a favour and had conferred their electoral privileges on the princes; hence also the attempt to set up in Tuscany a sort of vassal state of the Holy See, the interventions in the disputes between Aragonese and Angevins in Naples, and between Capetians and Plantagenets, and finally the institution of the jubilee at Rome in 1300. The trouble was that the pope failed to evaluate properly the strength and ambition of the French monarchy, and he made the mistake of asserting the weightiest principles in connection with trifling incidents.

THE CONFLICT BETWEEN BONIFACE VIII AND THE KING OF FRANCE

A first clash occurred by reason of the king's need of money. In 1294 and 1295 he demanded of the clergy payment of a two-year tithe—originally intended to finance the crusades—and of a tax of one-fiftieth on Church revenues. The financial immunities of the Church were at stake; the pope was their guarantor, since the councils of 1179 and 1215 had made the taxing of the clergy conditional upon his prior consent. Boniface recalled this fact on two occasions in 1296; he thought it right to refer to an enmity of long standing between clerks and laymen and to hint that he might support France's enemies, the King of England and the King of the Romans. Philip the Fair riposted by complete prohibition on the export of gold and silver coin, so as to paralyse the working of the pontifical fiscal system; the anonymous author of a "Discussion between a clerk and a knight" maintained that "even before there were clerks, the King of France had the keeping of his kingdom and could make regulations in it". Matters remained there; the French clergy had no interest in entering into conflict with the king and came to an arrangement with him: it used the rebellion of the Count of Flanders as a pretext for asking Rome's permission to grant a subvention to Philip the Fair. Boniface promptly admitted (1297) that in a case of pressing need—of which the king himself would be the judge—a contribution could be levied on Church properties. And to show the benevolence of his feelings towards the house of France, he canonized Louis IX.

It was the second encounter that produced a general exposition of theocratic doctrine, a heated dispute and the resort to force; the privileges traditionally accorded to the clergy were once more at the bottom of it. The Bishop of Pamiers, Bernard Saisset, had been imprisoned; Boniface VIII not only claimed to have him handed over to his own jurisdiction but also, at the end of 1301—in a state of over-enthusiasm, perhaps, after the recent jubilee celebrations—explained that, as sole head of the Church and of Christendom, he was, through God, raised above peoples and kingdoms. He took his stand on this assertion to enunciate precise grievances, concerning the oppression of subjects and monetary transactions no less than attacks on ecclesiastical liberties, and to convene in Rome a council of French prelates and university teachers to go into the question of how to reform the government and conduct of the king.

Theologians—Henry of Cremona, Giles of Rome, James of Viterbo—drew up all the arguments that had long been advanced in support of the theocratic position into a coherent political philosophy that Boniface expressed forcibly in the Bull *Unam Sanctam* of November 18th, 1302: rejecting any attenuation in the power of the Holy See, he equated those who supported the independence of the temporal power with the Manichean heretics who believed in the coexistence of two divine Principles. Bull asserted the supremacy of the spiritual power over the temporal, the right of the pope to depose erring kings, and the doctrine of the "two swords", the spiritual and the temporal.

Since an ideological debate was joined and the Christian people were involved, the royal party, in its turn, appealed to public opinion: before the representatives of the various "orders" of the kingdom a royal counsellor, Peter Flote, refuted the Roman claims. Publicists criticized the papacy's interpretation of texts and exalted the power of the king to whose authority, inside the kingdom, the Church was subservient. The unknown author of a "Contradictory Examination of the two Theses" and the Dominican John of Paris in a treatise on "The Royal Power and the Pontifical Power" went to great lengths to map out the respective domains of the two powers and outline the way they could collaborate; they rediscovered the idea of antiquity, that the state is a self-sufficient natural organism.

The French government, however, preoccupied by events in Flanders, replied with moderation to the reproaches made to it by Cardinal John Lemoine. Conversations might have begun and a formula for agreement been found if Boniface, believing victory at hand, had not rudely threatened to take action against the king unless he received his immediate submission, and if Philip had not come round to a daring plan proposed to him by William Nogaret. This fanatical adviser, whose family had been in trouble with the inquisition in the south of France, suggested taking the offensive by means of an attack on the pope's person; on the pretext that his election to the pontifical throne had been illegal, that he practised disgraceful vices and that the faith he professed was not even orthodox, the plan was to have him arraigned before a general council and, meanwhile, to hold him. While a gathering of nobles approved the plan, and letters were sent off to the cardinals and princes, Nogaret crossed into Italy. He had the whole-hearted support of the great Colonna family, who were pitted against that of Boniface VIII in a remorseless hostility; they had been overcome in a war that was turned into a crusade, and had been deprived of their property and titles. Nogaret, learning that, on September 8th, 1303, the feast of the nativity of the Blessed Virgin, the pope intended to publish a Bull excommunicating the King of France and releasing his subjects from their duty of loyalty, marched upon Anagni where Boniface was staying. It was Sciarra Colonna that led the operation; he took the palace of the Caetani on the 7th; he insulted the pope and struck him. Nogaret announced frigidly that until the meeting of the council he was constituting himself Boniface's keeper. But the people of Anagni, terrified at the idea that Sciarra Colonna was perhaps going to kill the head of the Church and that they might be accused of complicity, drove out the intruders on September 9th; an armed escort brought the pope to Rome where he died, a completely broken man, on October 11th.

The French king and his advisers were not satisfied with the disappearance of their adversary; they had been unable to discredit him living, they intended to degrade his memory. This cardinal point in the policy of the strongest state in the West brought the most formidable pressure to bear on the Holy See over several years—it was impossible for the pope to convene a solemn session of the Church to blame one of his predecessors at the request of a secular power without creating a tremendous precedent and debasing the Roman See.

Boniface VIII's successors avoided the issue. Benedict XI removed all the censures that Philip the Fair had incurred and pronounced a general absolution, from which, however, he excepted Nogaret, who was summoned to appear before the pope's tribunal. But Benedict died very suddenly, on July 7th, 1304. His place was not filled until June 5th, 1305, by the Archbishop of Bordeaux, Bertrand de Got: Clement V annulled the two main Bulls in which the theocratic doctrine was laid down, he undertook to summon before him the accusers and defenders of Boniface, he had the evidence collected, he commanded that the acts which the king considered contrary to the interests of his crown should be deleted from the registers of his chancellery, he acknowledged that Philip had acted in the interests of his faith, and he gave explicit absolution to the accessories to the Anagni outrage, with the reservation that Nogaret should submit to a penance. Finally, in 1311, he persuaded the king to entrust him with the responsibility for winding up the case, which he did by burying it; in 1313, when canonizing Celestine V, he took the precaution of doing so under the name of Peter di Murrone in order to suggest that the renunciation had been really valid.

The honour of the Holy See had been saved. As a matter of fact, from the moment when the French government had opened the trial of the Templars the case against Boniface's memory had been no more than a means of blackmail. To counter this manoeuvre, Clement V, who was of a wavering and peace-loving disposition, had been led to make very heavy concessions.

THE TRIAL OF THE TEMPLARS

Bertrand de Got was not a member of the Sacred College; he had learned of his election while on a pastoral visitation of Poitou. He decided to have himself crowned before crossing the Alps, and to use his stay in France to improve relations between the Holy See and the King of France, and also to bring about a reconciliation between the latter and the King of England, at odds over the homage owed by the Plantagenet to the Capetian for the duchy of Guyenne. As a Gascon Clement V judged himself to be better placed than anyone to straighten out this difference of opinion and free the forces of the two monarchs for a resumption of the crusade for which, at that time, numerous plans were being made.

So the cardinals and the officials of the curia joined the pope in France, and he was crowned at Lyons. Philip the Fair attended the ceremony; the strong influence he had from this moment over the pope, the seriousness of the problems he raised, the influence of the French and meridional cardinals introduced into the Sacred College, and the scarcely encouraging news of the situation in central Italy henceforth kept Clement from making up his mind to return to his "own see", as he never failed to call the Roman Church, towards which he showed a real interest and a real generosity. A new meeting with the king was arranged at Poitiers, but was delayed by the pope's illness until the spring of 1307. It was at this point that Philip was to break the news of his intentions concerning the Templars.

This Order, which was both religious and military, was sworn to the defence of the Holy Land; on this count, it was one of the institutions of Christendom. To ensure for it the necessary recruits and resources, it had set up commanderies at the centre of the vast domains it possessed throughout Europe; its castles were protected by the privileges enjoyed by ecclesiastical establishments, and had appeared appropriate places for the deposit of money belonging to laymen; from the time of Philip Augustus the French monarchy had made use of the Temple foundation in Paris for this purpose. The Order's many establishments and its experience in transferring funds to the East had led the Templars to undertake financial dealings on a large scale—they had quickly become bankers. And after the loss of their last strongholds in the Holy Land that is all they were. Did they serve any purpose? Was the best thing not to merge them with the other military Orders, and notably the Hospitallers? The question was the more insistent in that rumours were circulating, fed by the mystery surrounding the Order's practices, that cast doubt on the orthodoxy and morality of its members.

The king decided to act. Whatever one may think of the procedures he resorted to, he was probably motivated at the outset by good intentions. He was convinced that the accusations made to him were well founded; he adopted them as his own, and passed them on to Clement V. The latter thought it his duty to take the case in hand; on August 24th, 1307, he ordered an inquiry into the Order.

What Philip expected was an expeditious procedure, followed by a verdict of guilty. On October 13th, he had all the Templars in France arrested—including the Grand Master, James of Molai—and their belongings sequestrated; his officers undertook the interrogation themselves, extracted confessions—if necessary by torture—and then handed the unhappy knights over to the inquisitors. Clement V, wishing to regain the initiative, ordered all Christian sovereigns to imprison the Templars and sequestrate their property; then, having cancelled the powers of the inquisitors, he reserved the case to himself.

Philip the Fair returned to Poitiers in May, 1308; strengthened by the approbation he had received from an assembly of notables, and using the charges against the memory of Boniface VIII to create a scare, he had a full indictment of the Order read out in the middle of the consistory, and arranged for a few carefully chosen Templars to repeat, before the pope, their shattering confessions. Clement V resigned himself to allowing diocesan commissions to examine the cases of individual Templars, while instituting pontifical commissions to examine the charges against the Order itself; a council at Vienne, on the Rhône, on imperial soil but on its frontier with France, would decide the fate of the Order.

While awaiting this ecumenical assembly, which did not take place until October 16th, 1311, the pope established the curia at Avignon, which belonged to the King of Naples, Count of Provence, a vassal of the Holy See; and he gravitated between that town and various residences in the county of Venaissin, which had become a papal possession by confiscation from the counts of Toulouse, marquises of Provence, as a result of their complicity with the Albigenses. The two investigations—papal and episcopal—followed very different courses in France and outside it. Under pressure from the French authorities, a council of the province of Sens (which at that time included the diocese of Paris) sent more than fifty Templars to the stake after they had retracted their original confessions; at the same time, before the pontifical commission, the Order had found energetic defenders. Except in Cyprus, whose king profited from the chance to work off a grudge, the inquiries turned out favourably for the Order and its members: only a few witnesses could be found to accuse them—in Provence, the kingdom of Naples and the Papal States. So the council, when it was presented with the transcripts of the evidence, decided that the trial of the Order should be begun afresh and the evidence in defence should be presented before the council.

Once more, the King of France intervened. He came to Vienne. The great majority of the prelates concluded that the best course was to give up the idea of a new and conflicting investigation; they handed over to Clement V the responsibility for delivering judgement. The pope's decision was not a judicial one, but that of an administrator acting in accordance with the overriding interests of the Church: in 1312, he limited himself to recording that the honour of the Order had been called in question and that its confiscated property was in danger of being misappropriated. He therefore pronounced the suppression of the Order and the transfer of its property to the Hospitallers.

It is true that he had been ruled by fear of the King of France, but he had managed to avoid adopting the viewpoint of the accusers and leaving them the material profit from the disappearance of the Temple. A tragic occurrence proved, however, to what point the prestige of the Holy See had sunk. The officers of the Order were judged by cardinals; they had been sentenced to life imprisonment when James of Molai, the

Grand Master, and Geoffrey of Charnay, recovering themselves, proclaimed that the Order was innocent; in consternation, the cardinals handed the newly relapsed prisoners back to the provost of Paris, a royal officer, while they deliberated; Philip the Fair and his council profited from the circumstances to send the two men straightway to the stake. According to tradition, the death of the pope and the king in the same year, 1314, was to be attributed to the summons issued by James of Molai, from amid flames, citing them to appear before the judgement-seat of God.

Seen in conjunction with the humiliation at Anagni, the trial of the Templars struck people's imagination and revealed the weakness of the pontifical power in the face of secular forces. In the history of western Christendom, these are in fact major events, showing clearly that a certain political conception was shattered and at the same time delivering a rude blow to the institution that embodied it. This did not, it is true, prevent the Holy See from reviving its theocratic propositions concerning the Empire or carrying still further the centralization of the Church. But these were threadbare and insignificant triumphs. The attacks came with increasing frequency and the effective authority of the pope never ceased to decline.

THE HOLLOWNESS OF IMPERIAL PRETENSIONS

Since 1250, there had been no holder of the imperial title. Kings succeeded one another in a dismembered Germany, the playthings of their electors, feeble masters of "a complex whose parts did not add up to a whole". To the west, beyond the Rhine and the Alps, they could not prevent the encroachments of the King of France. In Italy, in the midst of continual struggles between the lords and the communes, there was no one now to defend their cause save the party of the Ghibellines. They had, moreover, shown themselves incapable of helping their supporters, while the opposing party of the Guelphs had found a leader in the Angevin prince whom the papacy had installed in the south of the peninsula and who, solely dependent on the Holy See, symbolized the very negation of the imperial idea; in 1314, Robert of Naples proposed that the Empire should be left indefinitely vacant, and Italy and Germany finally sundered. Beyond the traditional territorial limits of the kingdoms of Germany, Italy and Arles, the Empire carried no weight: legists were proclaiming loudly that the King of France was "emperor in his kingdom", and Philip listened favourably to the suggestion of cornering the Empire for himself or a member of his family.

The glamorous imperial tradition and the unifying temporal principle that it represented were not forgotten, however. Its temporary eclipse was not to mean its disappearance. For Boniface VIII, the emperor was the highest individual in secular society, on whom the other princes depended but who, in his turn, was subordinate to the pope. When he recognized Albert of Austria as King of the Romans, hence candidate for the Empire, the pope had obtained from him adherence to his theory and an oath of loyalty. In 1308, despite the manoeuvring of Philip the Fair, Clement V took measures not to impede the election of Henry of Luxemburg. He hastened to confirm it and promise to crown Henry emperor at Rome. He judged, doubtless, that the restoration of the Empire was an advantage for the political stability of Christendom and the restoration of his own authority in Italy. On June 29th, 1312, three cardinals placed the diadem on Henry VII's head.

But the emperor had a lofty conception of his mission and his prerogatives; he agreed not to stay at Rome without the pope's permission, but he intended to take charge of the proceedings against Robert, King of Naples, who was making war on him; he strove to convict Robert of felony and treason; on April 26th, 1313, he condemned him to death, released his subjects from their oath of loyalty and handed his kingdom over to the King of Aragon, who already held Sicily. He was preparing to execute the sentence when he was carried off by a fever. In actual fact, Henry VII's ambitious endeavour showed up the weakness of the imperial power; by wanting to set himself up as arbiter, Henry had only envenomed the struggle between the Guelphs and the Ghibellines. He had been incapable of being more than the head of a party: at Rome he had been obliged to arrange his coronation at the Lateran because his enemies had not been dislodged from the district around St Peter's. No less Platonic, in these circumstances, was the pontifical doctrine expounded by Clement V in two decretals of March 14th, 1314: he argued that the emperor, at the moment of his coronation, swore an oath of loyalty, like any vassal, and had no right to judge the King of Naples; "we annul [Henry's conviction of Robert]," he wrote, "in virtue of the undoubted supremacy that the Holy See enjoys over the Empire, of the right that the head of the Church possesses to administer the Empire when there is no emperor, and by that plenitude of jurisdiction that the successor of St Peter has received from Jesus Christ, the King of Kings and Lord of Lords".

It was at this time, nevertheless, that the vision of the Empire took on one of its most impressive forms. Engelbert, the Cistercian Abbot of Admont, pointed out about 1308 that a unified temporal power was necessary to ensure the peace of mankind, and that this rôle devolved on the Empire, whose authority Christ himself had acknowledged during his earthly life, by submitting to the requirements of the census and to the jurisdiction of Pilate. But it was left to Dante to make the philosophical justification of the Empire in ringing terms. Its domain and that of the Church were distinct; God had established Peter and Caesar directly under him, had created two suns of equal splendour; the Church was the spiritual association of the human race, the Empire the framework within which were contained all men and all things in time. The two institutions, autonomous but concordant, corresponded to the double nature of man: one provided for his eternal beatitude, the other for his earthly felicity.

The poet had hailed in Henry VII the providential hero who, by restoring peace to Italy, would finally realize the potentialities of the Empire; he accused the papacy of his day of betraying the true interests of the Church—he relegated Clement V, with Nicholas III and Boniface VIII, to the eighth zone of Hell, among the simoniacs; he submerged the Gascon pope in floods of wrath for selling his throne to the French monarchy. But it was at the moment when Henry VII was exacerbating the divisions of Italy and vanishing without having accomplished anything, that Dante developed his political ideas in his treatise *On Monarchy*. More even than the theocratic vision of a unified Christendom, the idea of the universal Roman Empire was decidedly out of touch with the realities of the situation; it was becoming an ideal mode of being for the West, a hope of unity, a messianic vision.

CHAPTER V

THE AGE OF THE
AVIGNON POPES

If the pope felt the need to recall his supreme rights over the world, despite its unpropitious development, he had even better reasons for strengthening his hold over the Church. This was only natural on the part of the legists who at that time occupied the Apostolic See and finally completed the transformation into a system of government of the growing powers that their predecessors had claimed. But it was at Avignon that the capital of the pontifical monarchy was set up.

AVIGNON AND THE PONTIFICAL MONARCHY

The town had never been regarded by Clement V as more than a halting place. But John XXII, his successor, who had been its bishop, found it convenient to set up a temporary residence there: at the intersection of the route that ran along the valley of the Rhône with the long-established road linking northern Italy and Spain, through the south of France, the city's geographical position was, taking everything into account, more advantageous than that of Rome, which was not at the physical centre of the Christian West. It was not the kings of France who kept the popes prisoner—the town belonged to the count of Provence, and was acquired by the Holy See in 1348. But it offered a security that Italy seemed unable to guarantee.

The popes thought that it was not possible for them to return to Rome until the country had been pacified. John XXII tried to break the power of the Visconti and the Scaliger families, lords of Milan and Verona respectively and the mainstays of the Ghibelline party, so as to be able to get back to Bologna, or else to set up in the north a vassal state corresponding to the kingdom of Naples in the south, and then to establish order in the Papal States. He failed. Benedict XII (1334–42) believed in the virtue of a conciliatory policy, with no better results. Clement VI (1342–52) once more favoured force, but he lacked resources and the city of Rome was led into rebellion by Cola di Rienzo. Innocent VI (1352–62) saw that in order to succeed great sacrifices were necessary; he gave the Spanish Cardinal Albornoz the necessary means to reconquer central Italy.

These pontiffs devoted between forty and sixty-three per cent of their budget to the Italian enterprises; they never forgot that they were bishops of Rome. But, in the meantime, first Benedict XII and then Clement VI thought it wise to build a double palace at Avignon, covering an area of some 7,500 square yards and stoutly defended, in order to house the organs of their administration. It is altogether natural that the administration corresponding to the rôle of absolute monarch played by the pope in Church affairs should have shown itself loath to move.

A Franciscan contemporary of John XXII, Alvaro Palayo, asserted that "Christ was with the Church, the Church with the pope"; for him, it was on the pope's authority that the Church rested. The laws of Clement V (the Clementines) and those of his successors (the *Extravagantes*) completed the codex of canon law. The Avignon popes made great efforts to repair the shortcomings of ecclesiastical organization; after the Council of Vienne, which had sought to resolve various disputed ques‹ tions, and whose canons had moreover been promulgated by Clement V himself, they made concern with reform their per‹ sonal responsibility—publishing, for instance, constitutions for the chief religious Orders. They were the sole masters of the hierarchy: Clement V and John XXII, on learning of the conversions effected by the mendicant Orders in Mongolian Asia, raised Pekin and Zaitun to the status of archbishoprics, to which they appointed a Franciscan and a Dominican; they consecrated bishops whom the metropolitans were to use according to the needs of the communities they were responsible for. They could cherish the illusion that an immense territory, stretching from the shores of the Black Sea to northern China, was in a fair way to being evangelized; what new vistas would have been opened up before the Church by an acquisition on this scale if, shortly after the middle of the fourteenth century, the Ming revolution in the Far East and the victories of the fanatical Muslim, Tamerlane, had not destroyed the efforts of the missionaries? In the West, however, the papacy's authority over the Church was manifested in two ways: by its disposing of a very great number of benefices, and by the setting in motion of a very efficient system of taxation. Benedict XII, who was moderate in his exercise of his rights over benefices, conferred or promised four thousand in a little more than seven years; he had almost complete control over recruitment to the body of bishops, as is shown by the fact that in France the cathedral chapters elected freely only nine bishops out of a total of fifty-eight vacancies filled. A flood of petitions flowed in to Avignon—more than ten thousand have been preserved from the first year of Urban V's reign. As for the taxes, which were raised on the revenues of benefices conferred by the pope, or simply claimed by him instead of going to the bishops who normally collected them, they necessitated the setting up of a network of "collectorates" and the collaboration of Italian commercial and banking firms, the only organizations capable of effecting continuous and complicated movements of funds.

At Avignon, a highly complex administrative machine centralized and controlled all the matters which the pope had ensured should fall to his cognizance: in the chancellery, in the penitentiary, in the treasury which was still called the Camera, and in the court known as the Rota, some 250 to 350 officials worked. The cardinals advised the pope, who called them together in the consistory, they served as legates, and managed a number of important departments. Squires, sergeants and ushers provided for the protection and policing of the world of the curia. Although the pontifical agents received regular salaries, paid in cash, or disposed of the income from benefices, and although the patriarchal way of life of the old curia was vanishing, the pope maintained a lavish household; he took in members of his family, he entertained princes, he fed the poor, and to complete his court there were his domestic establishment and his almonry.

How was it that such a papacy, conscious of its rights and duties and well organized, aroused so much criticism? In the first place, it gave the impression that it was using its prerogatives to favour the clients of the reigning pope: Clement V's new nominations to the college of cardinals had been Gascons; his successors came from Quercy, the Pyrenees and Limousin— they surrounded themselves with compatriots, they practised a shameless nepotism. Frenchmen from the south piled up Church offices and Church revenues. The Italians, who had taken a generous share of them at the end of the thirteenth century, expressed the most burning indignation—but all those who failed to profit from the share-out joined in the chorus. In parallel vein, irritation was produced by the partiality the pope showed towards the King of France; and it is true that the papacy went as far as making over to him the collection of taxes on church property and advancing him huge sums of money, but France's help was indispensable to all the temporal projects of the popes, and it was the country that bore the brunt of their policy regarding benefices and finance. Secondly, the personal qualities of some of the popes were not all that could be desired: John XXII was a fine administrator, but he allowed himself to express some strange opinions about the state of souls immediately after death; Clement VI's taste for luxury provided matter for astonishment—the palace at Avignon owes its biggest apartments and the greater part of its pictorial decoration to him, but people were unaccustomed to seeing the Vicar of Christ living like a powerful lord. Urban V is the only one of them to have been beatified. Finally, the Avignon period had in it something disquieting, something unlooked-for. The popes had often left Rome, but they had never been away from it for so long. That was the Church's spiritual capital, whatever administrative importance Avignon might have acquired. That alone was the place where it was possible to proclaim the jubilee by which the faithful could profit from the treasure of indulgences stored up by the Church; by founding this new practice in 1300, Boniface VIII had made plain the unique position held by the city in which the apostles Peter and Paul had shed their blood; this fact was recognized by Clement VI, who proclaimed another jubilee for the year 1350, once more at Rome—but by so doing he implicitly admitted the unsatisfactory basis of the Avignon papacy.

RESISTANCE TO THE PAPACY

A fresh conflict of papacy and Empire sparked off a whole series of revolts. As had already occurred, the German electors, unable to agree, had elected two kings in 1314, Frederick of Hapsburg and Lewis, Duke of Bavaria. As soon as he acceded, John XXII made it clear that until the candidatures had been examined, and one of the elected sovereigns confirmed and authorized to receive the imperial crown, the Empire was without a head: its "government, its administration and its supreme jurisdiction devolved on the Sovereign Pontiff to whom God, in the person of St Peter, has committed the right to command both in heaven and on earth". Thus was stated, at the outset, the theocratic doctrine from which the Avignon popes never departed. It was confirmed by theologians.

Meanwhile, Lewis was getting the better of his rival and, feeling himself strong enough in Germany, he undertook to enforce his rights over Italy. He sent a vicar to Lombardy, who re-formed the Ghibelline league and forced the papal legate to raise the siege of Milan. John XXII then drew up an accusation of Lewis, whom he branded as a usurper; in 1324, he excommunicated him, released his subjects from their oath of loyalty and put an interdict on any territories that accepted his power. But in several manifestos, Lewis proclaimed that election by the princes put the King of Germany in possession of all his prerogatives, including the government of the Empire, and that confirmation and the grant of the imperial crown were merely formalities that the pope could not refuse.

It was at this point that Lewis of Bavaria's protests received support from two movements of thought which formally denied the basis of pontifical authority, as it was understood and exercised by John XXII. Marsiglio of Padua and John of Janduno, in their *Defensor Pacis*, saw in the Church no more than a name to distinguish those who held the Christian faith in common; according to them, it was the state, emanating from the body of citizens, which should satisfy the material, spiritual, and indeed the strictly religious, needs of men: they handed over to the state the task of choosing and maintaining the clergy. The pretensions of the papacy took on the appearance of a scandalous usurpation.

Marsiglio, who had been rector of the University of Paris, and whose thought was guided by Averroism, making a complete dichotomy between the domains of faith and reason, waxed passionate: "To unmask the lying of those bishops, I rise as a herald of truth and I cry to you. . . . Do you see the immense depredations wrought by all those Roman bishops with their hordes of clerks and cardinals bent on sowing falsehood from their black books?" And he accused the popes of starting impious wars which caused the death of the faithful "with hatred or evil in their hearts". In 1327, John XXII condemned the essential arguments of the *Defensor Pacis*; Cardinal Peter Roger, who made a detailed study of the work, noted 240 errors in it, and when he became Pope Clement VI, he branded Marsiglio as the worst of heretics.

The intrepid theorist had taken refuge with Lewis of Bavaria, where he had found a band of Franciscans who, in May, 1324, had inspired the accusation of heresy made against John XXII in the declaration of Sachsenhausen.

It will be recalled that, in the Franciscan order, the

"Spiritual" faction had never ceased to agitate against pontifical claims to interpret the rule of the founder. Persuaded of
the providential value of their opposition, they had defied the
severest strictures and refused all compromise. John XXII
persecuted them: in Provence, Languedoc and Catalonia, the
recalcitrant went to the stake; those who escaped—the Fraticelli—hid in the heart of the Apennines, or in Sicily or some of
the remoter parts of Spain, awaiting the end of the world. Was
the pope anxious to settle once for all the dispute about
poverty? Did he think that the distinction between property
and the use of property amounted in practice to no more than
a piece of verbal juggling? As absolute master of the hierarchy
and discipline of the Church, who would not concede that a
religious rule could not be subject to amendment, he made over
to the Friars Minor in 1322–4 the ownership of all the property
that had fallen to the Order or been given to it; and he further
declared that Jesus and the apostles, while living in poverty,
had exercised, in common and individually, the right of ownership: those who denied this were advancing a heretical opinion.
The Minister-General of the Franciscans, Michael of Cesena,
who obeyed with reservations, was summoned to Avignon and
treated with scant consideration. He thereupon decided to have
the pontifical opinions examined by William of Ockham who,
at the same time, was the subject of an inquiry by the theologians of the curia. He was not the man to feel any partiality
for papal authority, and he declared to Michael of Cesena that
John XXII's Bulls were "full of so many assertions that were
heretical, erroneous, foolish, stupid, chimerical, senseless, harm-
ful to the true faith, contrary to morality, to natural reason, to
experience and to brotherly charity..." that he "could not
remember ever having met a short treatise by a heretic or a
pagan which so mingled errors and truths".

Michael and William fled from Avignon and joined Lewis
of Bavaria at Pisa. The latter had proceeded to action: on
January 17th, 1328, at St Peter's in Rome, he had received
the imperial diadem from Sciarra Colonna, Boniface VIII's

assailant, representing the Roman people. In his presence, "the priest James of Cahors who styles himself John XXII" was proclaimed a heretic and his prerogatives forfeit; on May 12th, a Franciscan Spiritual, Brother Peter of Corvara, was elected pope; Lewis put the fisherman's ring on his finger and invested him with the temporalities of the Roman Church; then he was crowned a second time. The case argued in the *Defensor Pacis* seemed victorious: Marsiglio of Padua was appointed imperial vicar in spiritual matters.

The sequel to these spectacular gestures was a sorry one: the pope and the emperor had assumed attitudes that neither had the effective means of maintaining. The anti-pope was quickly abandoned by his patron, besought forgiveness, and ended his days comfortably as a prisoner at Avignon. Lewis of Bavaria was powerless to maintain his authority in Italy, but kept his control over Germany, although the Holy See went on stubbornly disputing his legitimacy up to his death in 1347. Marsiglio of Padua faded out of the picture; Michael of Cesena and William of Ockham were confined to the Franciscan monastery at Munich. It was obvious that the struggle had been pointless, anachronistic; if they had agreed to neglect their doctrinaire prejudices—the pope who desired the pacification of Italy so as to return, and the emperor who was chiefly interested in having his power in Germany recognized—they would have been able to come to an arrangement. For all that, on the elevated ideological plane, the debate had had a quality of greatness about it: the champions of both sides had once more, notwithstanding the changes in the world, expressed the aspiration towards Christian political unity. On the other hand, Marsiglio of Padua, who had occasion to acknowledge the emperor's right to break even the bonds of matrimony, had set on foot a new and ambitious philosophical conception of the state; the Friars Minor, in revolt, intent on discrediting the Holy See by accusing it of heresy, reproached it unremittingly with yielding to a rabid desire for power through its interventions in secular matters; William of Ockham explained in his successive treatises how the separation of the spiritual and the temporal should be brought about. There can be no dispute that it was a certain vision of Christendom that was shattered in the second quarter of the fourteenth century.

THE WEST IN THE MIDDLE OF THE FOURTEENTH CENTURY

Politically and juridically, fragmentation triumphed: the West was made up of a multiplicity of diverse cells sharing out among themselves the prerogatives of sovereignty; kingdoms, principalities, districts, towns, communities of all sorts, lived their own life within a network of compacts defining their respective status. William of Ockham had set the pattern by studying "the power and the rights of the Roman Empire"; he was followed by any group that founded its law, positively, on customs and privileges and a rationalizing propensity to define the area of its autonomy.

Thus the Empire took on a Germanic form. Clement VI had once again, in 1346, excommunicated Lewis of Bavaria and proclaimed his privileges forfeit; he had organized the election of one of his friends, Charles of Moravia, who had given precise pledges; after the disappearance of Lewis, the theocratic conception of the Empire had seemed to triumph. But it was precisely Charles IV who showed its emptiness for all to see. When Petrarch invited him to pacify Italy, he replied by referring to the chronic disorder in the peninsula, and said that any attempt to restore a rule that was universal in character was merely visionary. He came down into Italy for his coronation, but wherever he went he restricted himself to confirming the existing authorities and turning his favours into money. In Germany he promulgated in 1356 the celebrated document known as the Golden Bull, which regulated the composition of the electoral college charged with the appointment of the sovereign, and the procedure to be followed: there was no allusion in it to any intervention whatever by the pope—

whether to administer the Empire during a vacancy or to invest the elected candidate with his powers. He sanctioned the independence of the imperial power along lines opened up by the declaration of the princes at Rense and the constitutions of Lewis of Bavaria in 1338. And in 1376, during his own lifetime, he had his son Wenzel elected and crowned King of the Romans, in order to ensure his succession.

Within the frontiers of Italy, left to its own devices, papal influence was no more respected than the emperor's. The kingdom of Naples was now separated from the island of Sicily, whence it had proved impossible to dislodge the Aragonese; after the death of its king, Robert, in 1343, the kingdom entered a long period of disturbances under its new ruler, Queen Joanna: the Holy See's strongest support was weakening, while the power of the seigniorial states of the north was growing. The divisions between factions were beginning to follow less the old Guelph–Ghibelline lines, and more frequently *ad hoc* political considerations: barons and cities of both persuasions had come together in 1332 in the League of Ferrara to counteract the plan to found a new kingdom for John of Bohemia.

The ties of vassalage which, momentarily, had seemed to provide the papacy with an opportunity to formulate the policies of the kingdoms, were now no more than an outworn symbol. On coming to the throne Edward III of England had paid the arrears of tribute, but after that he paid nothing more for thirty-three years; when Urban V demanded payment, the king referred the matter to Parliament in 1366: the Lords and Commons, with the clergy concurring, released their sovereign from the obligation to pay feudal tribute, on the grounds that John, who had neither consulted the nation nor even respected his coronation oath, had no power to bind his successors. This constituted a unilateral repudiation and abolition of the vassal relationship between the Holy See and England.

The popes had never been wholly successful in deflecting the kings from their calculations of private interest; they had nevertheless been able to turn their attention towards Christendom's grand enterprise, the crusade. Now, the very legality of their intervention was in question.

It was at this point that the feudal dispute setting the King of France against the King of England, who was also the Duke of Guyenne, flared into war—the one that we call the "Hundred Years' War". Believing that his mission was to establish concord between the Christian princes and win them to service of the crusade, the pope could not remain indifferent; but he had no hope of making his voice heard, either by setting himself up in judgement on sin—to condemn the one and absolve the other—or by preaching loving kindness. The only courses open to him were either to keep on despatching legates in the hope of bringing the two adversaries closer together, or else to offer to arbitrate. But it was not as one endowed with a power superior to that of the two monarchs that he came on the scene; he acted only as an intermediary, anxious to have his good offices accepted, as a private person who was friendly to both parties: this was the approach of Boniface VIII in 1298, and of Clement VI in 1344. The former succeeded for a while, the latter not at all. The princes were not of a mind to tolerate interference that seemed to them unwarranted; they took the decisions themselves about hostilities and negotiations, and if they appealed to the pope it was only so that his moral prestige should guarantee the agreements discussed and concluded by them. So the war dragged interminably on, punctuated by truces, but always threatening, and stultifying any other great undertaking.

At the time of the Council of Vienna, 1311–12, and again in 1336 and 1363, the Kings of France and the energetic King of Cyprus, Peter of Lusignan, seemed ready to take charge of a great effort to regain a footing in Syria. The popes levied taxes and fitted out galleys. The results were absurd, amounting to no more than the installation of the Hospitallers in Rhodes, the formation of some small squadrons, the capture of Smyrna, a few cruises in the Archipelago and a Cypriot raid on

Alexandria. Harried by the Ottoman Turks and by his domestic enemies, the Byzantine emperor, John V Palaeologus, came in 1369 and made his submission to the Roman Church; a poor success, however, for the Holy See, seeing that the Greek clergy did not obey him, and that he was held for insolvency by his Venetian creditors.

Indeed, the kings were disposed to accept only the spiritual authority of the papacy; they sought to gain control of the churches within their states, by limiting their judicial privileges, by subjecting them to taxation and by supervising the appointment to benefices. The King of France derived great advantages from his good relations with the pope; his claims were not formulated in tactless terms. But the Englishman had nothing to gain by circumspection; on the grounds that he was protecting the rights of ecclesiastical establishments, Edward III, putting himself forward as the supreme patron of the benefices of the kingdom, obtained from his Parliament, in 1351 and 1353, measures that restored the prerogatives of the patrons of benefices and imposed serious limitations on appeals to the papal courts. The era of national Churches was dawning.

RETURN OF THE PAPACY TO ROME

There were some who considered that the abandonment of Rome was the cause of the decline in papal authority. Italians regarded the period on the banks of the Rhône as a betrayal: Dante, at the beginning of the Avignon period, breathed the lament of an Italy left without a leader, and the anger of the faithful who saw Rome's institution confiscated by Frenchmen whose only thought was to feather their nests. Petrarch, inflamed by the inspiriting memories of ancient Rome awakened in his day by Cola di Rienzo, portrayed Avignon as a city of perdition. These invectives, by their passion and their eloquence, have greatly contributed to the idea of a "Babylonian captivity"—although the Italian patriotism of that period was only the vision of a few intellectuals, and Petrarch was not above soliciting the favours of the French popes. The issue should be put in mystical, rather than national, terms. St Bridget of Sweden had arrived in Rome in 1349, seeking approval for her foundation of the Order of Saint Saviour; she was present at the jubilee the following year; she understood the spiritual greatness of the city. In her *Book of Revelations*, in which she described the tasks to be accomplished in Church reform, social renovation and efforts against unbelievers, she showed that the impetus could come only from Rome. St Catherine of Siena echoed her words: after 1374, especially, she repeated that blood alone purifies, that Christians must offer themselves in sacrifice, and that the Church had no higher mission to offer them than the crusade; to the pope, whom she venerated as "Christ on earth", but whom she addressed with an inimitable mixture of tenderness, arrogance, respect and violence, she pointed out that return to Rome, "his proper place", was the very condition of respect for his office.

But it was not these inspired voices whose influence was decisive. Cardinal Albornoz's campaigns seemed to have re-established order in the Papal States; Avignon had become less safe since unemployed bands of mercenaries were infesting the south of France. Urban V, in the face of advice from the King of France and from the great majority of his cardinals and courtiers, embarked at Marseilles in the spring of 1367. The agitation in Italy upset him; a renewal of hostilities between France and England caused him to recross the Alps, and he died at Avignon in 1370. Gregory XI immediately took up his plan again, but its implementation was held up by his desire to put an end to the great war in the West which was making any plan for a crusade pointless, as well as by the operations against the Visconti of Milan, the revolt of Florence and uprisings in the pontifical towns. The pope was forceful beneath a frail exterior; he put Florence under an interdict, required the princes to drive out Florentine merchants and cancelled the debts owing to them; he recruited mercenaries; through a cardinal he replied to the brother of the King of France who was trying to hold him back: "Has anyone ever seen a kingdom well governed in the absence of the prince? Certainly, if the King of France departed from his kingdom and went to Greece, his would never be well administered. I cannot conceive of his domains being pacified if the pope does not reside in his own see." On January 13th, 1377, he at last entered Rome.

Was the papacy about to fulfil the expectations of its impatient servants, right the wrongs done to God, in accordance with the ardent entreaties of St Catherine? Would it apply itself to reform of the Church, although maintaining the shibboleth of the crusade? In fact, its position was weak, disputed, threatened. There was, all the same, thanks to the gesture of the return to Rome, a promise of renewal when Gregory XI, worn out, died on March 27th, 1378. And then the great scandal occurred.

CHAPTER VI

THE CHURCH RENT ASUNDER

There had already been papal schisms; usually, there had been one shepherd of unimpeachable legitimacy, who was opposed only by a candidate of the emperor, a mere tool in his hands. In 1378, it was in the very bosom of the Church of Rome that there arose two heads who, in good faith, could both believe in the validity of their appointment and mission. Their fate depended on the support or the hostility of the princes: the rôles assigned to the two parties in the theocratic thesis were precisely reversed. Under the twofold influence of practical action and reflection, the Church's very constitution was reappraised.

THE GREAT SCHISM OF THE WEST

The citizens of Rome did not intend to let the future pope once more forsake his see. As they could not but entertain doubts about the intentions of the sixteen cardinals present in Rome—which included no more than four Italians to twelve Frenchmen—they clearly demonstrated their wishes by organizing threatening processions through the streets. The cardinals quickly reached agreement, and named the Archbishop of Bari, Bartholomew Prignano. But they had to wait on his acceptance; the mob grew more and more excited, finally breaking into the conclave; the bewildered prelates threw the papal mantle over the shoulders of their aged colleague, Cardinal Tebaldeschi, who was acclaimed by his Roman compatriots. When Prignano finally arrived, they enthroned him and acknowledged him under the name of Urban VI.

This was a bitter experience for those cardinals who, for several decades, had been seeking, obstinately but unsuccessfully, to superintend the administration of the Church and bind the man they elected to their conditions. And the behaviour of the new pope towards them was an even more bitter mortification. Brutal, insolent, and extravagant in speech and manner, he spoke of nothing save of bringing the cardinals to heel, of giving the Sacred College a completely new composition, and of reducing its wealth. The cardinals began to ask themselves whether the election had been altogether regular—its course had, as everyone knew, been marked by a series of disturbing incidents. On the pretext of getting away from the intense heat of the Roman summer, thirteen of them arrived in Anagni, where they declared the election of Prignano void, as it had been made under threat of violence. Joined by three Italians, they crossed into Neapolitan territory and, on September 20th, 1378, at Fondi, for all the world as though, once they had denounced him, Urban VI no longer counted, they nominated one of their number, Robert of Geneva, who took the name of Clement VII.

The rivalry of the two popes straightway took on a political colouring: the decisive question was to know which way the nations would opt between them. Queen Joanna of Naples supported the Fondi candidate; the King of France came round to him in the hope that his decision would persuade many other sovereigns. But the only ones who followed him immediately were Scotland and Savoy, while his English cousin made haste to recognize Urban VI to whom the Emperor Charles IV also remained faithful. During the years that followed, the map showing the two "obediences" was filled in: the Clementine gained Castile, Aragon and Navarre, the Urbanist the kingdoms of northern and central Europe and of Portugal. In certain areas, the lords and the inhabitants opted for different sides, and rival bishops disputed the sees. The doctors drew up arguments in academic form, the publicists adduced proof on proof, legates organized contradictory propaganda. There was as much calculation and good faith, as many politicians and saintly characters, in the one camp as the other.

Clement VII thought he was in a position to rush matters; he unleashed troops of mercenaries on Rome. They were broken up. Then, on June 20th, 1379, he took refuge at Avignon. The Church had two heads, who had lost no time in setting up two colleges of cardinals, two administrations which, in their respective obediences, followed the same methods in exploiting benefices. Clement VII interested the younger French princes in his cause, first Louis of Anjou, whom he made heir to the kingdom of Naples, then Louis of Orleans, whom he married to the daughter of the Duke of Milan, Valentina Visconti; he hoped that if a Valois was installed in Italy he would open up for him the path to Rome. These efforts failed. The schism was deepening: Boniface IX replaced Urban VI, Benedict XIII Clement VII.

For a long time the University of Paris, mindful of its former position as the light of western Christendom, was preoccupied in trying to heal the division of the Church without resort to force; but the French government, committed to the support of Clement VII, had imposed silence on it. It was not until 1394 that it could organize a consultation and deliver its opinion; it concluded that three possible ways were open: a simultaneous renunciation by the two popes; compromise or arbitration; and the calling of a universal council.

In a momentary agreement with the King of England and the King of the "Romans", Charles V of France sought to persuade the two pontiffs to stand down. Being unsuccessful in this, he withdrew from the Avignon obedience, without thereby bringing unity to the Roman. What a peculiar arrangement was this withdrawal of 1398, which cut the Church of France off from the pope and gave the responsibility for its functioning to the king, the provincial synods, the bishops and the traditional patrons of the benefices. It is also irrefutable testimony to the discredit that had overtaken the Holy See, and to the novel aspect that the Church universal was in danger of assuming.

Abandoned by France, forsaken by his cardinals, Benedict XIII stood firm; he withstood the siege of his palace, blockade and diplomatic intrigue; in March, 1403, in disguise, he fled from Avignon and called on the Count of Provence to protect him. Impressed by his courage and embarrassed by the unwonted attitude they had adopted, the national Churches which, like that of France, had deserted his obedience, returned.

It was hoped that the two pontiffs would now make the ending of the schism their main preoccupation. In 1407, they seemed to have made up their minds to meet, but they avoided coming within less than twenty leagues of one another. Once more, France left the obedience of Benedict XIII.

In each camp, the cardinals held the view that, since they were responsible for the schism, they held the means of healing it: what an opportunity this would be to show the prerogatives of the Sacred College! Clementines and Urbanists met and called a council at Pisa; in 1409, the two popes were deposed by the council, and the cardinals elected Alexander V. Here was but a third pope! For him he had the greater part of Christendom, but the Urbanist, now Gregory XII, still had faithful followers in Italy, southern Germany and Poland; and Benedict XIII was supported by Aragon and Castile.

Sigismund, who was King of the Romans and virtual emperor, obliged John XXIII, Alexander V's successor, to call a general council in the imperial town of Constance. The position of the Church was frightening.

An effort must be made to understand the mentality of the Christians of those days. An entire generation had known only a Church rent asunder, popes who preached crusades against one another, governments that haggled over the price of their loyalty. The enduring demand for purity that was contained in the desire for "reform of the Church" had been betrayed by popes or princes eager to exploit ecclesiastical establishments or find posts for their clients. The image of the Church had grown hazy; the equilibrium that the preceding three centuries had given it had been lost. Some German burgesses declared that they were only interested now in their priests, that the pope meant nothing to them and that it was up to the clergy to decide for one or the other. They, at any rate, did not contest the mediation of the priesthood, the value of the sacraments or the articles of faith. But it is easy to understand how others, scandalized by the turn events had taken, gave an ear to the appeals of the heretics.

HERESY

Despite the vigorous efforts of the Avignon popes, the old heresies had not disappeared: Waldensians who labelled the Church an imposture held on in the upper valleys of the Alps and southern Italy, and won recruits among peasants and artisans across the whole of central Europe; Brothers of the Free Spirit, who professed a pantheistic vision of the world, recruited adepts in the pious Beghard communities of the Low Countries; Fraticelli, heirs to the Spiritual Franciscans, waited among the mountain tops for the triumph of the Spirit; the Cathars, more or less extinct in the south of France and Italy, made up a thriving Church in Bosnia, which survived expeditions sent against them by the kings of Hungary.

But the disorder within the Church engendered new heresies. They differed from the summarily expressed heretical doctrines of the eleventh and twelfth centuries in being expounded by academic theologians who, strong in their method and their knowledge, attacked the foundations of the constitution and belief of the Roman Church; in a simplified form they spread among the people, where they served to nourish and justify religious, social and national claims.

John Wyclif was one of Oxford's most brilliant products. His knowledge of both Testaments and of St Augustine was faultless. When the King of England resisted the claims of the

Avignon pope, he demonstrated learnedly that God had dispensed authority to all those who, on the earth, held a fragment of command; if the clergy misused its property, the prince had the right to take it from them and even to accuse the pope. Wyclif was used by the government in negotiations and the bishops, far from condemning him as Gregory XI hoped, merely asked him, in 1378, to give up advancing arguable and disquieting propositions. The master, however, had discovered the principle on which to base all criticism: "The Holy Spirit", he declared, "teaches us the meaning of the Scriptures as Christ revealed it to the apostles." Encouraged by the spectacle of the schism, he asserted that no text from Scripture authorized the pretensions of the pope and the monarchical form of his power; he waxed indignant over the cupidity of the secular clergy and the encroachments of the mendicant Orders. He saw in the Church only the wholly spiritual society of the souls to whom God had revealed his truth and, through his grace, indicated the path of salvation. He no longer believed in transubstantiation; he honoured the Blessed Virgin and the saints, but thought it idle to invoke them; he strongly rejected indulgences and pilgrimages; rather than penance, a mechanical matter of rites and juridical exactions, he favoured the unfettered movements of a heart that feels itself sinful and repents.

Wyclif would not acknowledge that priests had any other vocation than to recall these truths and give the spectacle of a life of poverty. He sent "poor priests" through England, leaving translations of the Bible behind them. And at the moment when he was driven from Oxford, when his ideas were censured by theologians and he was ending his life in his calm but isolated parish of Lutterworth, his teaching was finding favour in popular circles: it was invoked by the peasants who, incensed by the harshness of their lot, the rise in prices and the burden of taxation, threw themselves on abbeys and manors, and even carried the Tower of London in 1381; it animated the small groups of Lollards who rose up in protest against the civil order and the ecclesiastical system. After the accession of Henry of Lancaster in 1399, the bishops obtained the assistance of the king in hunting the heretics.

But another, and remarkably more virulent, centre of heterodoxy was developing in Bohemia. Having a Czech population but forming a kingdom included within the boundaries of the Empire, this land ruled by the house of Luxemburg was coming under Germanic influence. Waldensian infiltration and apocalyptic expectations of an imminent end to time had found a receptive soil in the Slav mentality, which had been alienated by the collaboration of the ecclesiastical hierarchy in the policy of Germanization. At the end of the fourteenth century, academic teachers were exalting the dignity of the lay member of the Church, the sole authority of the Bible, the exclusively spiritual character of the Church. Jerome of Prague acquainted them with Wyclif's chief works. They eventually found a vantage-point from which to address their compatriots, when the little Bethlehem Chapel in Prague was reserved for preaching in the Czech tongue.

John Hus spoke there in 1402. Educated in the Faculty of Arts, of which he became the rector, and ordained to the priesthood, he found without difficulty, in commenting on the Gospel, the condemnation of clerical cupidity and disputes. He was protected by the archbishop; King Wenzel satisfied him to the extent of reversing the German preponderance in the university where henceforth the Czech "nation" had three votes in debates against one for the three other "nations", Bavaria, Saxony and Poland. With the election of a third pope, confusion in Bohemia reached its peak: the mob pillaged church property; the archbishop, at the end of his patience, ordered Wyclif's books to be burnt and excommunicated John Hus, but he was unable to have his sentence promulgated and preferred to withdraw. The king forbade all adverse comment on papal authority. Meanwhile, the Pisan pope initiated a canonical examination of the Czech doctor; he anathematized him in 1412.

Far from abating, Hus's audacity increased; in a state of exaltation he wrote: "the people that walked in darkness have seen the great light of Jesus Christ. They no longer have ears for anything save the Holy Scriptures. . . . But the Lord has not completed the work which he entrusted to my brothers and me; he will give strength to the evangelists." There was a profound humility in him, and the conviction that he was accomplishing the will of God: when he learned of his condemnation, he appealed to Jesus Christ, the sole head of the Church. Although the king banished him from Prague, he continued to preach freely; the number of his followers (Hussites) increased; he now embodied the conscience of a whole people. He stood up for the claims of the country communities against the lords; and he held it allowable to receive communion under both kinds.

THE COUNCIL OF CONSTANCE (1414–18)

It was anarchy within the Church that the Council of Constance had to face. But was this even a council? From the beginning of the twelfth century there had been held some of these general assemblies of Christendom, but they had been summoned, presided over and directed by the pope. When Philip the Fair, and later Lewis of Bavaria and the rebellious Franciscans, had demanded recourse to a general council, they had based their appeal on the necessity to judge a pontiff who was, in their eyes, heretical and unworthy. Canonists, comparing the structure of the individual Churches with that of corporations, where power was shared between the head and the members, had clearly revealed tendencies scarcely compatible with the absolute dominion of the pope, but they had not drawn the conclusions of their observations. Marsiglio of Padua and William of Ockham, in their turn, had developed their analysis systematically and shown that authority lay in the body of the faithful represented by the council; but they had spoken as heretics, condemned by the papacy. And yet the importance of such assemblies was increasing in the kingdoms,

From the beginning of the schism there was a new vigour in the propounding of conciliar theory: it was no longer just a matter of taking an exceptional step to resolve an inextricable crisis; with the great Paris doctors, Peter d'Ailly and John Gerson, the council made its appearance as the supreme legislative tribunal which must meet periodically and to which the pope was responsible for his government.

The manner in which the Council of Constance was organized from the earliest days of the year 1415 threw into even clearer relief its revolutionary character: the doctors of theology and law were admitted on the same footing as the abbots and bishops, and the vote was taken by "nations" (French, German, Italian, Spanish and English). In April the council's rights were clearly formulated: the council, representing the universal Church, was directly inspired by God; every member of the Church, including the pope, had to obey it in matters of faith, the suppression of the schism and the reform of the Church; any resistance was unlawful. The council proceeded straightway to the great problems referred to it.

Though it was intent on reducing and limiting the authority of the pope, it was by no means prepared to recognize that of individuals. On May 4th, 1415, forty-five propositions drawn from the works of Wyclif were condemned, and the Bishop of Lincoln was ordered to scatter the remains of his body. On June 5th, the public arraignment of John Hus was opened; he defended himself on the charge of denying transubstantiation and the efficacy of the sacraments, but he refused to disavow the promptings of his conscience and to "scandalize the people [whom he had] led in the path of truth"; on July 6th, he was sentenced to loss of rights and burning at the stake. His companion, Jerome of Prague, seemed to weaken; he abjured his errors; but when they tried to drive him too far, he recovered himself and was put to death on May 30th, 1416, as a relapsed heretic. But the nobles of Bohemia were organizing themselves into armed leagues. The priests remained faithful to the reformers and expelled from their churches those who approved of the council; they continued to administer Holy Communion under both kinds. The University of Prague was not afraid to assert the orthodoxy and sanctity of John Hus.

Still, the unity of the Church was re-established. The council had demanded the renunciation of the three rival popes. Only Gregory XII, representing the Urbanist obedience, brought himself to abdicate. John XXIII, who was supported by France, submitted only after being deposed. As for Benedict XIII, in whom the old Clementine party was represented, he shut himself up in Peñiscola on the Catalan coast and went on proclaiming his legitimacy until the day of his death. On November 11th, 1417, the cardinals, reinforced by thirty delegates from the "nations", put an end to the schism that had lasted thirty-nine years by unanimously electing Martin V.

But the council had no intention of restoring the "plenitude of power" to the pope. A month previously, it had decided that the council should meet periodically; it had decided the terms of the new pope's profession of faith and drawn up a list of abuses to be put right, which consisted almost entirely of the practices of the Holy See in matters of benefices, finance and legal administration. Martin V appreciated that he would have to satisfy some of its demands; he revoked irregular dispensations, gave up collecting the revenues from benefices declared "vacant in the court of Rome", forbade the arbitrary levying of tithes, and promised the nations not to interfere for the space of five years in the collation of ecclesiastical offices. The council, whether out of weariness or a feeling of satisfaction, broke up on April 22nd, 1418.

THE POPE, THE COUNCIL AND THE NATIONAL CHURCHES

The reform of the Church and the eradication of the Hussite heresy in Bohemia were two urgent necessities. But it was not clear which authority would take charge of the movement. The pope was not resigned to his lowly status. The council, which had proclaimed its rights, was to sit regularly. The kings, with their hands on the religious institutions, were only too happy to justify their old ambitions for dominion by the theses of their doctors on the Church's constitution. These three forces struggled for supremacy for more than thirty years.

Martin V returned to Rome on September 29th, 1420. He made the restoration of the Papal States his main preoccupation. It was a staggering task; the holy city itself was a field of ruins and a den of thieves. It was not enough to reconquer the ground with the services of a mercenary leader—a *condottiere* —it was necessary to hold on to it. The pope set up the members of his family. But Eugenius IV, elected in 1431, was forced to abandon Rome and take flight over the water, in pitiful circumstances, in 1434. It was only nine years later that he was able to return to his capital, after undertaking a systematic reconquest through a churchman with the gifts of a great general, Cardinal Vitelleschi. This had been an expensive policy. The wise regulations that Martin V had published in 1425 on the cardinals' style of living, the residence of bishops and abbots and the raising of unjust taxes remained a dead letter. The Holy See did, however, achieve a signal victory: the extreme danger in which the Ottoman Turks had placed what remained of the Byzantine Empire had led the eastern emperor, once more, to approach the Church of Rome; conversations took place in a council convened by the pope, which sat first at Ferrara and then at Florence. In 1439, union was proclaimed; the Greeks admitted that the Holy Spirit proceeded from the Father and the Son, and that the pope was the head of the universal Church. An admirable fresco painted by Benozzo Gozzoli for the chapel of the Medici palace still recalls, in the form of a procession through the Tuscan countryside, the long-awaited reconciliation. On this occasion, the primacy of the Roman pontiff was solemnly defined: he was "the true vicar of Jesus Christ, the head of the whole Church, the shepherd and the doctor of all Christians". Unfortunately, three weeks previously, another council meeting at Basle had deposed Eugenius IV.

In virtue of the decisions taken at Constance, Martin V was obliged to call a council at Pavia in 1423; he took measures to make it ineffectual; because of an outbreak of disease, he transferred it to Siena and then, because of the small number of members, he declared it to be dissolved. But in 1431 Eugenius IV was faced with a council meeting at Basle; relations were strained from the first; the pope wanted to try his predecessor's device of transferring the council, but the council opposed the move: it was its turn to threaten the pope with suspension. It had adopted a seal which represented the benediction of the Most High extending without discrimination over a pope, a cardinal, prelates and doctors; it abolished the reservation of benefices to the profit of the see of Rome, limited the right of appeal to the curia, prohibited the levying of certain taxes and called the collectors before it to present their accounts. It was concerned above all with putting an end to the religious war that was devastating Bohemia. Revolution had been raging there since 1419. Sigismund, who was already master of Germany, had inherited the kingdom of Bohemia as a result of the death of his brother Wenzel; he represented the forces of Germanic and Roman oppression, and it was against him that the Czech population, nurtured in the memory of the national martyr, John Hus, had risen up. In eleven years, five crusades failed. The Bohemian Church allowed its members to communicate under both kinds, authorized unrestricted preaching of the Bible and refused to let its clerics possess property. But dissension was growing among the rebels: the moderates, who avoided any imprudent theological assertion and strove to avoid a breach with the Church, were opposed by the Taborites, who admitted no other mediation than that of Christ between God and man. Sigismund and Cardinal Giuliano Cesarini, who had witnessed the defeat of a new expedition, saw that it was better to negotiate with the moderates and leave them to settle accounts with the extremists. The civil war actually effected the defeat of the Taborites in 1434. The negotiations that had been initiated in the Council of Basle reached fruition in the signing of the Pact of Iglau, July 5th, 1436. The Czechs were given the right to maintain their eucharistic rites and to go about their preaching in their own way, provided they were licensed by their superiors; the properties confiscated by the nobles had to be returned to the religious establishments.

The council had thus accepted the autonomy of a national Church. In its eagerness to abolish the practices of the papal monarchy, it was itself inciting the Churches to recover their "freedom". It sent ambassadors to the assembly that the King of France had called at Bourges; it requested the adoption of its decrees in the kingdom; the Pragmatic Sanction of July 7th, 1438, turned them into a law of France; the right to dispose of benefices and their revenues was taken from the pope, and the chief Christian state in the West acknowledged the supremacy of the council and the need for it to meet periodically. The following year, analogous measures were adopted in Germany. England had long been challenging the claims of Rome. Under the supreme authority of the ecumenical assembly, a new Church structure was coming into being. The concern with reform was not neglected; with a praiseworthy sincerity, the Bourges assembly had adopted measures designed to improve the standard of worship. But, in fact, although the Churches were apparently freed and restored to the ancient canonical traditions, they were in danger of rapidly coming under the thumb of the princes: the text of 1438 even authorized the king to employ "gentle and benevolent prayers" for the appointment of his candidates to bishoprics and abbeys.

Eugenius IV had disavowed the Council of Basle and called another meeting at Ferrara. He was suspended, and answered with excommunication; in 1439 he was declared heretical and deposed; the council elected the Duke of Savoy pope, and he chose the name Felix V. But the new schism was kept within narrow limits; Eugenius IV and later Nicholas V devoted their efforts to depriving the council of German protection; by promising the imperial crown to Frederick III they recovered some rights over the German Church; and they managed to achieve the dispersal of the last delegates who were holding on at Basle. In 1449, Nicholas was enabled to give proof of moderation: Felix V abdicated and was appointed a cardinal; dignitaries deprived of their rights were restored to office; the measures taken against the council were annulled, the paper on which they had been inscribed being destroyed.

Theoretically, the council had not disavowed its ambitions; but in fact, it was the papacy that triumphed. The Spanish theologian, Juan de Torquemada, undertook afresh the demonstration of the sovereignty of the Holy See; its rôle as dispenser of graces was given prominence by the jubilee year of 1450.

CHAPTER VII

AN ERA OF DISQUIET

The long crisis that convulsed the Church was not the only thing to bewilder people and overthrow every form of temporal Christian unity. Between the first quarter of the fourteenth century and the middle of the fifteenth, the western world was beset by so many ills that its material, emotional and intellectual foundations were shattered.

It was the presentiment of this moral fragmentation of Christendom that the poet Rutebeuf had expressed as far back as 1295 in his *Lament of Holy Church*: "I say the world has nor base nor root."

In next to no time, disaster followed disaster. A first epidemic, of dysentery, advanced from Scandinavia into central France in 1316. In 1347, a ship coming from the Crimea brought the plague to Sicily, whence it made its inexorable way across Europe and into England; it annihilated the mendicant communities in the south of France; it caused the death of more than half the inhabitants of the towns of Tuscany; it cut the population of England by a good third; as the Black Death it reappeared in 1358, 1373, at the end of the century, in 1431 and 1438. Famines, the result of freak weather and poor harvests, found men as helpless when confronted with the problem of hunger as before that of disease: in 1315, the large towns of Flanders were decimated. And lastly there was war, with its black sequel of pillage, destruction and violence: war between the King of England and the King of France—interrupted, it is true, by truces, but lasting all told much more than a hundred years; war between the kingdoms of the Iberian peninsula; war between the lords and communes in Italy; war between Poland

and the Teutonic Order, now based in Prussia; war between the Christians of central Europe and the Ottoman Turks; and, within the frontiers of individual states, war between parties and classes. Everywhere, there was fighting; the areas that escaped during actual hostilities were sacked by the unemployed mercenaries after the armistices.

The population curve took a downward plunge; whole tracts of land went out of cultivation; villages were abandoned; the economy was in a state of recession over a long period; the coinage was debased; there was no stability in prices; the masters of the labour market tried to hold wages steady, while doing their best to raise the revenues, rents and tribute moneys from which they benefited. Western man had never been free of material difficulties; but now they were felt all the more cruelly for coming after a period of expansion and relative peace.

MORAL DIVISIONS IN THE WEST

Various kinds of rudimentary solidarity came into being on the basis of common hatreds, common afflictions and common dangers. The social classes confronted one another. In the towns, the workpeople strove to wrest from the well-to-do middle classes the control of municipal institutions, production and trade. The peasants were swept by waves of anger, they hurled themselves on the feudal manors and brought down savage reprisals on themselves. Struggles against a common foreign enemy led to the development of an awareness of nationality; the Hundred Years' War was not just a dispute between two royal houses, but the encounter of two peoples, the English and the French, and peace—as Joan of Arc so clearly saw—must come from a refusal by the former to meddle in the affairs of the latter. The Czechs in the University of Prague proclaimed that they must be "the first in the kingdom of Bohemia, as the French were in the kingdom of France, or the Germans in Germany". Whether in terms of a mere city, of a state as obviously artificial as the Burgundy of the Valois, or of a kingdom, patriotism was seeking adherents. It found support and a means of expression in the national languages. Though Latin might still serve for the liturgy, for teaching and the advancement of knowledge, national idioms, the slow creations of poets and prose writers, were becoming established, over the head of regional dialects, to translate the aspirations, the railleries or the histories of the different peoples. Wyclif and Hus advocated the translation of the Bible into English and Czech respectively. Public opinion was taken into account; the princes called assemblies to explain their policies and obtain support. The very universities lost their cosmopolitan character; they were founded ever more thickly, from Coimbra to Uppsala, from Catania to Louvain, from Cracow to Glasgow; the kingdom of Aragon alone contained Perpignan, Huesca, Lérida and Valencia.

The schools were from this time brought into politics. Because he was no more than the "King of Bourges", whose authority hardly went north of the Loire, Charles VII opened a university at Poitiers, but after he had recaptured Paris the English, who still held the west of France, founded universities at Caen and Bordeaux. The University of Paris strove to remain faithful to its rôle as Christendom's intellectual centre— it put out its views on the great schism of the West, it urged the setting-up of the councils of Constance and Basle, it gained acceptance for a new conception of the Church. But where it had formerly been the "elder daughter of the Church", it was dubbed "elder daughter of the king" by Charles V; most of its teachers rallied to the Burgundian party; it took part in the preparation and signing of the treaty of Troyes in 1420, under which the Dauphin was disinherited for the King of England's benefit; it directed the trial of Joan of Arc. Thus, once the English were driven from the capital, it lost its privileges.

Not even the field of artistic expression was free of the effects of upheaval, isolated experimentation and the ever more strongly defined reflection of individual temperaments. France lost her leading position.

THE INDIVIDUAL'S APPROACH TO LIFE

To Europe's external divisions corresponded an inner discord. There is endless evidence of the instability and excesses that characterize all unsettled periods.

Men aspired to a life of beauty and harmony: the upper classes were committed to the ideal of chivalry, with the astonishing prowess it called for on the part of the knight, so that he might win favour in his lady's eyes and his name be handed down to posterity. It was the ambition of every knight to be received into one of the orders created by the princes, with their impressive names: the Star, the Sword, the Golden Shield, the Garter, the Porcupine, the Greyhound, the Golden Fleece. Love was decked out in the same refinements as the noble career of arms; it had its subtle symbolism of rings, jewels, veils, presents and ladies' favours, and the debates in the "courts of love" presided over by the Burgundian dukes— so many elegant extensions of the courtly tendency to endue the strongest and most widespread of human emotions with style. All those who had the means to do so yielded to the temptations of luxury, embellished the surroundings of their daily lives; the houses of bishops, lords and merchants were better furnished, more comfortable and showed more opulence. Both men and women took more care over dress and followed the dictates of fashion. Court life developed at Paris, Naples, Budapest and around the Avignon popes.

Nevertheless, these same men were also capable of terrifying fits of rage, of violence, grossness and intemperance of all kinds. The nobles openly maintained their bastards. In the Florence of the Medicis sodomy was rife. The simplest and most praiseworthy sentiments were developed to excess—as in the case of the Flagellants who overran Germany, lacerating themselves in over-zealous penance. Similarly, those who heard St Bernardine of Siena's preaching at the beginning of the fifteenth century immediately threw away wigs and cosmetics, jewels and dice. The vow was transformed into a gratuitous wager: Benedict XIII, besieged in Avignon, swore not to shave until he was delivered. The religious and military Orders lost their original character, to become more like aristocratic clubs. Elegance in clothing was carried to such lengths that it ended up in shoes with upcurved toes, and the tall hennins that sat in unstable majesty on the heads of women.

In their anguished uncertainty about the morrow, people clutched in puerile frenzy at superstitions: anyone who had been to Mass was supposed to be safe for the rest of the day from all risk of blindness or apoplexy. People consulted necromancers; occultism flourished and magic spells were cast; witches were pointed out, and the inquisition carried out trials for witchcraft: Joan of Arc was accused of being possessed by a devil.

Men were haunted by pain and death. One of the most popular books of the fifteenth century was *The Art of Dying*, whose author explained that the dying man was beset by five main temptations—against which he recommended a firm confidence in God, the Blessed Virgin, the angels and the saints. The churches were filled with large, costly and sumptuous tombs. The great manor houses had their own private vaults. The generality of people were buried in the hallowed acre of the church cemetery; but later their bones were dug up and piled in charnel-houses—at the Cemetery of the Innocents in Paris they could be seen through wide apertures. Dead people were portrayed as dried-up bodies, both in the recumbent figures of funeral monuments and on the frescoes representing the Dance of Death. Art and literature made much of the "Tale of the Three Dead Men and the Three Living", in which three grimacing dead men reveal to three handsome noblemen the frightening passage from earthly glory to the inevitable decay of the grave.

Piety became a matter of urgency and pathos. It turned towards the Christ of the Passion and the Virgin of Calvary. It forced itself to re-discover the stages on the "Way of the Cross". It stood in contemplation before the group known as the *Pietà*, comprising Mary and her dead Son lying across her knees, at the foot of the Cross. The stage undertook to develop the tragic events of Holy Week; clerks and laymen together provided the actors in these "mysteries" which were staged on the parvises of the churches, followed with breathless attention by the entire population. From the midst of the suffering there arose a tender confidence in the God of goodness and his gracious, earthly Mother. People delighted in touching and ingenuous details of our Saviour's childhood; the Angelus became widespread, the *Ave Maria* was established in its definitive form, inspiring much Italian poetry; the rosary, called the Psalter of Our Lady, was widely said. But for all this, having no firm standard of taste, the age tolerated vulgarities in the miracle and mystery plays, and even in handbooks of devotion and along the pilgrim routes.

THE ANTI-CLIMAX TO INTELLECTUAL DEVELOPMENT

From the time when scholasticism had established itself thinkers, in St Anselm's fine phrase, had provided the spectacle of "faith in search of understanding". They might accord reason only a subordinate rôle, as in the Augustinian perspective adopted by the Franciscans; or they might, with the great Dominican doctors, think it possible to establish its frontiers; but they all believed that the human intellect was capable of reaching out and joining up with the teachings of revelation.

Already, in the first third of the thirteenth century, doubts had been expressed about the possibility of this grandiose ambition: Roger Bacon had invited men to be satisfied with observing and describing the world of sense. Another Friar Minor, John Duns Scotus, who passed through Oxford and Paris in the first years of the fourteenth century, established the elements of a synthesis quite different from that of St Thomas: his conception of the God of Revelation was so elevated that he renounced any attempt to understand a will that could only be totally free, and he put all his hope of finding God in the mystical transports of love. "God", he deemed, "has not revealed to men the truths that reason can reach; reason does not reach the truths revealed by God." Philosophy and theology were quite separate; it was quite enough for reason to study the realities of sense in themselves, without striving after an impossible concordance with the supernatural.

Duns Scotus' thinking was at all times profoundly religious. But the dissociation of reason and faith was pregnant with dangers. John of Janduno and Marsiglio of Padua, who denied any vocation peculiar to the Church, built the state up into a complete and perfect society. The masters of Padua revived the Averroist tradition that recognized only the truths that could be demonstrated by the intellect. The English Franciscan, William of Ockham, went even further: maintaining that man could grasp by his own efforts only what he apprehended through his senses, he concluded that general ideas, or "universals", existed only in the mind which fabricated them; they were merely so many words, having no reality. He was far from denying that there was a divine truth; he accepted in its entirety the message entrusted to the Church's keeping; but he declared that it was unintelligible to reason; God existed, but beyond the reach of rational theology and metaphysics, both of which he condemned as useless. The only thing a thinker could apply himself to was the observation of the particular—that is to say, experience.

On these critical bases, philosophical inquiry took two directions. On the one hand, it concerned itself with human capacities: did men enjoy free will? what certainties were they capable of acquiring? what sort of arguments did reason use? There was no question now of grace; man was mapping out his forces; his relationship with the supernatural world was thrown into the melting-pot, and morality assumed a relative character. On the other hand, the mind, sure of its tools, ventured on the development of practical knowledge; some of the corner stones of modern science were put in position at this time. Men interested themselves in the movement of bodies, the density of the earth and its position in space. These speculations, however, turned sterile. At the end of the fourteenth century, university teaching fell back on the digging-over of theses formerly propounded by the masters, and on interminable and futile discussions of formal logic; verbalism stifled authentic intellectual progress, or rather its subtleties seemed to take the place of it. While the teachers came together into a caste, while the colleges avidly acquired manorial rights and revenues, while the universities allowed themselves to be drawn into political squabbles, the fruitful period of scholasticism was coming to a close; the intellectual method of medieval Europe was being transformed into that caricature of itself which, full of pretensions but divorced from all efficacy, would provoke its adversaries to scorn. This disappointing outcome was further aggravated by the existence of two opposing schools: those who clung to the old method (*via antiqua*), and those who supported the new method (*via moderna*)—successors, these latter, to William of Ockham. John Gerson, chancellor of the University of Paris, who died in 1429, was conscious of a philosophical and theological schism.

The inability to establish true science was only offset by certain technical advances, among which were the making of somewhat improved maps, the erection of public clocks, the perfecting of locks in Flanders, the use of the dredge, the development of hydraulic bellows for furnaces, the appearance of the crank-and-push-rod mechanism, wood-engraving and, about 1440, the first attempts at printing. The intellect was not yet in possession of the resources that would have enabled it to come under the spell of scientific discovery. Rather, it was encouraged by the failure of philosophy to set out on the path of mysticism.

SCOPE OF THE MYSTICAL MOVEMENT

In the fourteenth and fifteenth centuries, the mystical movement became exceptionally widespread. By its very nature, being essentially concerned with the emotions, it was well suited to a world dominated by the forces of feeling; it was capable of firing a believing soul of whatever kind, the scholar's and the ploughman's, the man of action's and the monk's.

There was a mysticism of men of action. The indefatigable Franciscan missionary, Raymond Lull, reveals the secret of the ardour which, in 1315, led him to martyrdom, when he recounts in his book, *The Lover and the Loved*, the personal experiences by which he rose to the state of ecstasy. At the end of this same century, during which theorists laid down the principles of positive government, the humble Catherine Benincasa of Siena, who lived only on the charity of Christ, which was burnt in stigmata on her flesh, noted down the astonishingly precise dialogues in which our Lord reminded her of the great tasks awaiting a Christendom that was denying itself by its divisions. Joan of Arc's every action, so simple and so steadfast, drew its strength from the conviction that her voices were not misleading her.

There was a mysticism of philosophers. Richard FitzRalph, turning to Jesus Christ, declared: "Until I had you, who are the Truth, to lead me I had heard without understanding the tumult of the philosophers whose prattling was directed against you—the crafty Jews, the haughty Greeks, the materialistic Saracens and the ignorant Armenians ..." Peter d'Ailly averred that "the doctrine of Aristotle deserves rather the name of opinion than of knowledge". Outside the limits of Aristotelianism, a school of lofty speculation had developed. Master John Eckhart adopted the articulations of neo-Platonic philosophy to show that the human mind, not essentially differing from the divine Intelligence, had for its natural object to find God and lose itself in him. Was this not to compromise the rôle of prayer and the sacraments, the Church's mediation, the value of the redemption? Certain of Eckhart's opinions came under pontifical censure. Two other Dominicans of the same Rhenish district employed themselves in extracting the practical applications from the Master's doctrine: John Tauler and Blessed

Henry Suso taught how to observe God's commandments and participate in social activities, while drawing nearer to Christ in union with the Blessed Virgin. Another centre of mysticism came into being in the Low Countries. When his long life ended in 1381, Blessed Jan Ruysbroeck—who was called the "admirable"—left behind several treatises in which he described how the soul, after overcoming sin and renouncing the world of appearances, rises up, by lovingly imitating Jesus, to the contemplative life, at the heart of which it experiences ineffable satisfactions and draws the strength to overflow in works of charity. During the fifteenth century, speculative mysticism held a privileged position in the University of Paris: there were teachers who did not shrink from comparing the processes of the intellect, wearing itself out in ratiocination, with the virtue of that asceticism which, aided by grace, allows the soul to glimpse God.

There was a mysticism of the religious life. Reformers attempted, through an effort of love, to restore monasticism, which had suffered in its quality from moral laxity and the misfortunes of the time. The same reminder of the values of mortification, renunciation and prayer made itself heard in many Orders: among the Benedictines; among the Carmelites where, in Tuscany, the influence of St Andrew Corsini (1301–73) was felt; among the Dominicans, directed by Raymond of Capua, the spiritual heir of St Catherine of Siena; among the Franciscans, to whom St Bernardine of Siena and St John Capistran brought increasingly numerous groups of Observants, whose autonomy was recognized by Pope Eugenius IV; among the Poor Clares, finally, where St Colette, in 1434, successfully gained approval for the restoration of absolute poverty. In the mystical Low Countries, the honour for the greatest number of new foundations fell to the Carthusians, who were so austere in their spirituality and the conditions of their life; the Order acquired no less than a hundred new establishments in the fourteenth century. The teaching of the masters directly inspired new congregations: Gerard Groote, a friend and disciple of Ruysbroeck, laid the foundations of a federation of Canons Regular which spread from the abbey of Windesheim across the whole of north-western Europe. The movement spread far beyond the ranks of the regular clergy; as in the eleventh and twelfth centuries, it led laymen to seek for forms of life which would allow them to prepare their salvation in poverty, asceticism and brotherly service.

There was a mysticism of the humble. Tauler and Suso formed societies of "Friends of God". Under Gerard Groote, a few clerks, some students and some workpeople pooled their resources, copied books, gave catechism classes in the vernacular and prayed together; after his death these groups of Brothers or Sisters of Common Life multiplied. The communities of Beguines underwent their period of greatest glory: after a year's novitiate and six years of community life, the Beguines were entitled to live in small houses situated in a special enclosure; they spun and wove, tended the sick and met together for the Divine Office under the direction of a Mistress-General. Among many others, there are individual lives that stand out: John Colombini, in 1355, abandoned a thriving business in Siena; he accepted the humblest of existences, but his letters reveal the exalting vicissitudes of his quest for God. Beginning in 1413, an Englishwoman, Margery Kempe, recorded the extraordinary revelations that came to her from her mystical strivings. A Tuscan Dominican, one Brother Giovanni, seemed to be so at home among supernatural visions that people said his inspired paintings were the work of angels, whence his surname, Fra Angelico. On a simpler level, from the turn of the thirteenth and fourteenth centuries, thousands upon thousands of souls found repose in the naïve and touching meditations of Jacob of Voragine's *Golden Legend* and the *Little Flowers* of St Francis of Assisi.

The *Imitation of Christ*, which was composed at the beginning of the fifteenth century, probably in the Low Countries, exactly sums up this sense of a piety which, nurtured in the contemplation of Jesus Christ, finds its application in each circumstance of daily life. "What is the use of profoundly discussing the Trinity if we offend it for want of humility?" we read in this little book that is wonderful in the psychology and love it reveals. "On the last day you will not be asked what you have learnt but what you have done."

Thus was defined what its contemporaries themselves called the *devotio moderna*. Yet, as a culture it was wholly interior; despite its refinements it was not made to inspire the West with a collective feeling of Christendom. It was individual, it could not come under the supervision of authority and could easily stray into heresy. And what is more, isolated from the field of purely human knowledge, it was difficult to reconcile with other influences which were making a simultaneous appeal to men's minds.

HUMANISM AND THE RENAISSANCE

By seeking a better knowledge of the works of antiquity, through admiration of their style and recognition of their example, men were beginning to realize the potentialities of human genius.

The dominant figure in the first form taken by humanism was Petrarch (1304–74). He extolled the great men of Rome and the virtues that Plutarch had emphasized; he believed he had found in Cicero and Seneca the principles of a philosophical reawakening. He restored the prestige of the fair Latin tongue, and founded a tradition of pious admiration for everything belonging to Greco-Roman antiquity. It fell to Lorenzo Valla (1405–57) to transform humanism into a method of study and research. He created Latin philology, and was able to apply his critical mind to ascertaining precisely the meaning of pagan doctrines and to showing the Donation of Constantine for the forgery that it is.

The artists of Italy had never ceased to be aware of the forms of antiquity, so many vestiges of which lay all about them. In the Quattrocento—the fifteenth century—they re-discovered the secret of their perfection. Brunelleschi (1377–1446) profited from a long period in Rome to make a systematic catalogue of columns, pilasters, pediments and cupolas. Leone Battista Alberti made a detailed study of Vitruvius before writing his architectural treatise. Donatello took his inspiration from the statues of antiquity.

If any of these men had been accused of forsaking the Christian tradition, he would have denied it. They simply wanted to freshen it, to bring it new strength: the study of ancient models seemed to them the best means of promoting a "re-birth". The popes were interested in collecting Greek and Latin literary works; they were patrons of the humanists, and by their commissions gave a stimulus to artistic progress. Petrarch admitted that Seneca and St Paul had corresponded, and that stoicism was not incompatible with the Gospel. Boccaccio regretted having written the sceptical and ironical stories of the *Decameron*. The humanists of Paris, who were genuinely distressed by the great schism and faithful to scholastic principles, turned to mysticism in search of orientation and counted d'Ailly and Gerson their masters. Lorenzo Valla himself composed Fra Angelico's epitaph. Ghiberti, who worked with consummate artistry on the doors of the Baptistery in Florence, made use of Giotto, the painter of the Franciscan ideal. In the chapel of the Florentine church of Santa Maria del Carmine that contains scenes from St Peter's life, Masolino and Masaccio handled volumes and space scientifically to express an intense religious emotion.

And yet—what temptations accompanied this revival! Was the teaching of the Ancients any less valid than the Bible as a basis for morality? Did not the virtue that Plutarch glorified make suffering and renunciation look like symbols of decrepitude? Did the technical virtuosity of the artist not invite him to accord more value to formal appearance than to the real meaning of his work? Reading Luigi Marsili—who for the conversion of souls to the truth gives as much weight to the maxims of ancient poets and thinkers as to Biblical precepts—

listening to Lorenzo Valla's lucid demonstration that pagan feeling and the preaching of Jesus are incompatible, or seeing Donatello's wonderful nude statue of David, it is impossible to avoid a feeling of disquiet, not to wonder whether the unstable equilibrium between Greco-Roman heritage and Christian tradition will suddenly give way, and the former triumph.

Man, sure now of his abilities, tended to bring everything back to his own measure. Petrarch advised the "Solitary Life" as a means of cultivating one's personality in peace. His disciples withdrew into aristocratic country residences in order to debate their problems of ethics. Filelfo advertised himself shamelessly as teacher of Greek and commentator. The wealthy who built themselves palaces, who figured in the pictures they presented to churches, who employed artists to serve their comfort and their pleasure, grew accustomed to situating on the earth the immemorial dream of a better life. While divisions were rife in the world of politics and the social scene, the Christian was beset by the temptations of individualism, in either religious or humanistic form.

CHAPTER VIII

THE WEST AND THE CHURCH IN THE MID-FIFTEENTH CENTURY

It would be a mistake to regard the middle of the fifteenth century as the end of a world: the individualist and religious revolution of the Reformation and the triumph of Renaissance humanism were not clearly heralded. The fall of Constantinople before the Ottoman Turks in 1453 revealed no new danger, since for centuries Christendom and Islam had been condemned to a coexistence that was sometimes belligerent, sometimes peaceful, but always unstable.

But for all that, the changes went very deep. Henceforth, the West was no longer flanked by the eastern bastion of the old Empire. Domestically, barely emerged from a long crisis that was political, economic, social, ecclesiastical and intellectual all at once, it revealed a new physiognomy. We must now attempt to sketch its features and estimate the opportunities remaining to the Church at the latter end of the era traditionally called the Middle Ages.

A PROFOUNDLY CHRISTIAN CIVILIZATION

Religion was still an intimate part of the texture of individual and collective life. It remained so incontrovertible a social duty that religious observance was practically unquestioned: it was only very rarely that a person was denounced for not having communicated at Easter or for failing to attend Mass over a long period. Religion inspired the reflections found in family record books, the continuing popularity of pilgrimages, the production of manuals of devotion, the commissioning of works of art, donations and legacies; the confraternities increased in number, and their members indulged in devotional exercises, took part in processions, presented altar pieces and sponsored the production of mystery plays. The faithful now prepared themselves for communion by specially composed acts before communion. It is true that official records contain details of concubinage, adultery, acts of violence and usurious practices; the humanist, Enea Silvio Piccolomini, before becoming an assiduous prelate and, in 1458, the excellent Pius II, could announce with elegant irony the birth of a bastard and write that "in his day the greater number of reigning princes had been born outside wedlock". But unbelief was unknown; moral shortcomings and a scant consideration for the blunted weapon of excommunication could coexist in minds made up of violent contrasts, with a nearly universal belief in the Immaculate Conception of the Virgin Mary, a touching faith in the merits stored up by Christ in suffering and the sorrowful Mother of the Passion, a renewed confidence in the saints.

Artistic styles still subserved Christian ends, whether they remained faithful to the Gothic tradition, adopted a realist view of the world or were influenced by the classicism of antiquity. Everywhere churches or chapels were built or finished in the Flamboyant Gothic, one of whose most daring masterpieces is the choir of the abbey church of the Mont Saint-Michel, which was in fact completed between 1450 and 1454. When the pupils of Claus Sluter carved the tombs of the dukes of Burgundy in the charterhouse of Champmol, they surrounded them with weeping figures in the tragic convention. The spirit of observation and the technique of painting in oils were transfigured by the vision of the mystic when Jan van Eyck put the final touches to his *Adoration of the Lamb*, in 1432, for the cathedral of St Bavon at Ghent, and when—about

1452—Roger van der Weyden handed over to the hospice at Beaune his polyptych of *The Last Judgement*. In Florence, which occupied a leading position in the field of Italian art, the principal public works undertaken in the first half of the century were the cathedral, the campanile and the baptistery.

In the revival of letters and the arts which was manifested throughout the peninsula, the Church played a very large part. Rome was a mass of ruins when the pontifical court re-established itself there in 1420. The popes planned to make it a metropolis of learning and beauty. Once the schism was repaired, Nicholas V (1447–55) was able to set this great work in hand. He reconstituted a library which, immediately, was the most widely used in Italy. Not satisfied with finding places for the humanists in his administrative services, he deemed it worth while to commission them to translate all the classical works known at that time. He resolved to transform the area stretching from the Vatican Hill to the castle of St Angelo and the Tiber; following the example of Eugenius IV, he made a point of beautifying his palace, whither he attracted Fra Angelico and the young Benozzo Gozzoli; he decided to rebuild the old basilica of St Peter's, which still bore the venerable appearance Constantine had given it, and—prompted by Alberti —to put a portico in front of it that would look out on to a marble staircase, and a large open square into which would lead three streets lined with porticoes. He ordered the repair of the forty churches that constituted the "stations" of the liturgy according to the Roman Missal.

On a deeper level, Nicholas of Cusa, born in 1401 in the diocese of Trier and raised to the cardinalate in 1449, who by his intelligence, his authority and his energy was the dominant figure in the Church of his time, propounded a synthesis of the mystical tradition and the scientific or Ockhamist tendencies with the scholarly methods of the humanists. His prodigious culture embraced Plato and the Fathers, the speculations of the Arabs and St Bernard; he was favourable to the critical philology of Valla; he admitted that the same laws governed the movements of the earth and the heavenly bodies; he wanted the calendar reformed. In a series of treatises, often written in the form of dialogues, he laid it down that God was the end of all knowledge, that the world offered a sure but incomplete image of him, that metaphysical inquiry, scientific research and mystical impulse were all equally valid and led to him, in whom all contradictions were resolved.

THE CHURCH IN LIGHT AND SHADE

The papacy was the keystone of the Church. It had seemingly recovered its lustre. The crowds that flocked to the jubilee of 1450 bore witness to the fact that it was the supreme bestower of indulgences, the source of the hierarchy and the object of a devotion that St Catherine had the courage to extol in the darkest hours of the Great Schism. Nicholas V sent legations headed by Nicholas of Cusa into Germany and the Low Countries, by the Franciscan John Capistran into central Europe, by Cardinal d'Estouteville into France, and by Cardinal Bessarion —who came from the Greek clergy—to Bologna.

Nevertheless, the authority of the Holy See encountered limitations and inadequacies of every kind. A Czech baron, George Podiebrad, had taken charge of Bohemia, and in 1452 the emperor was obliged to recognize him as administrator-general of the kingdom. Nicholas V would have liked to suppress the advantages enjoyed by the Czechs since the Pact of Iglau in 1436, but neither John Capistran's threats of a crusade nor Nicholas of Cusa's efforts to bring the two sides to a conference could shake the determination of a sovereign and a people who were inspired by the memory of the Hussite wars. The union with the Greek Church that had been proclaimed in 1439 at Florence aroused exactly the same distrust in the East as had rendered all previous efforts of this kind barren. The celebrations held at Constantinople on December 12th, 1452, meant nothing; the eastern Empire vanished a few months later, and under the Ottoman domination the Christians of the

Balkans and Asia Minor rallied round their own priests and monks; they remained faithful to their rites and beliefs, breaking off all contact with the Roman Church which had been incapable of saving them from invasion. As far as the Russian Church was concerned, the attempts at agreement had met with no more success. A metropolitan, who to all intents and purposes was independent, resided in Moscow.

Church reform was carried out in a spasmodic manner. There was no problem of recruitment to the priesthood, but war and disturbances had seriously affected the clergy and its wealth. The value of Church property in northern Italy and many parts of France had slumped; shrunken incomes had encouraged such reprehensible practices as absenteeism and plurality of benefices held *in commendam*. Lack of education meant that the minor clergy were almost universally ignorant. Although the religious Orders were animated by a spirit of renewal, the response of the secular clergy to the needs of their flocks was inadequate. The school of grammar and liturgy run by St Antoninus in Florence, and the educational establishments maintained in the Rhineland and the Low Countries by the Brothers of Common Life were isolated phenomena. Of what profit was it to the pope to despatch legates and reject the supremacy of councils, if the more conscientious of the faithful, not satisfied with making fun of their priests, turned towards a wholly personal piety?

Moreover, under the encouragement of the sovereigns and the influence of conciliar theory, the national Churches were fond of invoking their "liberties". In 1448 the Holy See recovered the greater part of the rights over the Church of Germany it had lost nine years earlier, but in France among university teachers and lawyers it encountered a point of view that upheld the Pragmatic Sanction of Bourges as the charter of "Gallicanism", and its only hope of regaining some of its advantages lay in agreeing to share them with the king. Western Christendom had become the Europe of the Princes.

THE END OF CHRISTENDOM

The same Eneas Silvio who, as Pope Pius II, was to proclaim that the Roman pontiffs were "the masters of men and all that belonged to man" had made the realistic observation: "Each state has its prince, each prince has his private interests. . . . What mortal could bring about an understanding between the English and the French, between the Genoese and the Aragonese, between the Germans, the Hungarians and the Bohemians?" The Hapsburg, Frederick III, who bowed before Nicholas V on March 19th, 1452, to receive the imperial crown, was no more than an Austrian baron, practically without power or resources. The Holy See no longer counted on the Empire: it devoted its energies to gathering together its own States, in their disparity and anarchy, and launched into political schemes that made and unmade alliances across the face of Italy. Thanks to its adhesion, together with that of Florence and the kingdom of Naples, the peace of Lodi that had originally been concluded between Venice and Milan was in 1455 transformed into an "Italian League".

The powerlessness to bring about a great collective upsurge received its most convincing demonstration in face of the Ottoman threat. The Ottoman Turks had crossed over into Thrace in the middle of the fourteenth century; their raids had spread across the Balkans in a methodical manner; first Bulgaria then Serbia, after the battle of Kossovo (Polje) in 1389, had gone under. Momentarily recalled into Anatolia, where their sultan had been beaten at Ankara by Tamerlane in 1402, they had resumed their offensive only in 1438. They carried off Christian children, brought them up in the Muslim faith and made slaves of them, giving them, nevertheless, the possibility of splendid careers in the army or the civil administration. The honour and the burden of defending their territories against the Turks fell on the sovereigns directly threatened, since the kings of England and France were at war, the emperor had all he could do to gain recognition for himself in Germany, and the papacy was either disputed by various claimants or at odds with the council. The King of Hungary had managed to strengthen his forces with some French and English knights, but these latter would not listen to his advice and were wiped out at Nicopolis, on the banks of the Danube, in 1396. Joan of Arc's exhortations to effect a general reconciliation so as to launch a new crusade fell on deaf ears. It was Ladislas Jagiellon, King of Poland and Hungary, János Hunyadi, Voivode of Transylvania, and the Serb George Brankovich who, in 1442, threw the Ottomans back; they were joined by a small army, led by the papal legate, Giuliano Cesarini; the crusaders crossed Bulgaria and reached Varna on the Black Sea—but this time they were beaten. The Ottomans decided to have done; on May 29th, 1453, they entered Constantinople, where the last Greek emperor died a hero's death. He bore the appropriate name of Constantine.

Nicholas V proclaimed the crusade; in 1458, Pius II summoned a congress of Christian princes; in 1460, he decreed another general expedition; in 1463, he announced that he would take command in person. The kings shirked the issue in a scandalous manner. It was János Hunyadi who saved Hungary by freeing Belgrade; it was a local chieftain, Skanderbeg, who prevented the Turks from occupying the mountains of Albania. But the conquerors had taken up their positions on the Adriatic coast, they held Greece and the Archipelago, they liquidated the Genoese trading posts on the Black Sea. A few islands still held out—Rhodes, with its Hospitallers, Crete and Cyprus. Pius II arrived in Ancona to await the army promised by the Duke of Burgundy and the fleet that Venice was to fit out. He collected altogether some undisciplined gangs and a few sail. He died on August 14th, 1464, in the bitterness of irredeemable failure.

It was he who had asserted ten years before: "Christendom has no longer any leader whom it respects or is willing to obey; the titles of Emperor and Sovereign Pontiff are for it no longer anything more than names without reality, and those who bear them are in its eyes only vain images." Would it not have been truer to say that Christendom no longer existed? From Scandinavia to the tiny Muslim kingdom of Granada, from Ireland to Lithuania, Christian civilization still constituted the common patrimony of the nations; but to the extent that Christendom had assumed, during the Middle Ages, the form of a society able to unite, at least temporarily, under a single inspiration, its time had run out.

More seriously still, the area of medieval Christendom within which the papacy had pursued its unifying projects had, from the beginning, been limited to the West, since the eastern Churches had demurred. The history of the Roman Church, which by definition is universal, had been confused with that of a small number of peoples and a limited extent of territory. The Church had penetrated all forms of western life, but they in their turn had moulded the Church. The Church, charged with leading men of every race and every background to divine salvation, had, through historical necessity, shouldered the risk of being linked to a particular civilization, and of being known only through a temporary expression of its earthly destiny, that of Western Christendom. That is one reason for the tenacity of the Byzantine schism. Whatever changes later centuries may have brought about, the misunderstanding is not yet dispelled.

About the year 1450, however, this confusion was less important than another danger, within the very frontiers of the West. It was in this sector, precisely, that signs of reinvigoration were everywhere noticeable: the growth of population, technical advances, the revival of the economy, the increased importance of money, the strengthening of governmental powers, the new paths taken by writers and artists—all these things testified to an increase in vitality. When the expansion of the eleventh and twelfth centuries took place, the Church had managed to participate in it; now it seemed less capable of making its influence respected; religion seemed to have become an individual affair; the pope and the clergy no longer enjoyed the prestige that had formerly permitted them to supervise the development of civilization. If this possibility eluded the Church, was not her very future at stake? She had as yet no inkling that the Portuguese, exploring the Azores and Madeira, steadily making their southing down the African coast, establishing posts on the Gambia and in the Cape Verde Islands, winning the pope's acknowledgement of their right to the lands on the route they were seeking to the Indies—that these men were opening up a whole new field for her, and restoring her ecumenical dimensions.

THE CHRISTIAN WORLD TOWARDS THE MIDDLE OF THE FIFTEENTH CENTURY

SELECT BIBLIOGRAPHY

In this series: CRISTIANI, Léon: *Heresies and Heretics*; CANU, Jean: *The Religious Orders of Men*; d'ORMESSON, Wladimir: *The Papacy.*

Standard Histories:

The Cambridge Medieval History, Volumes IV–VIII, Cambridge and New York, Cambridge Univ. Press, 1911–36.

The Cambridge Economic History of Europe, two volumes, Cambridge and New York, Cambridge Univ. Press, 1941–52.

In *The Oxford History of England,* the following volumes:

POWICKE, F. M.: *The Thirteenth Century,* London and New York, Oxford Univ. Press, 1953.

MACKISACK, M.: *The Fourteenth Century,* London and New York, Oxford Univ. Press, 1959.

Works of general or ecclesiastical history:

BARRACLOUGH, G.: *Medieval Germany,* London and New York, Oxford Univ. Press, 1938.

BOISSONADE, P.: *Life and Work in Medieval Europe* (trans. E. Power), London, Kegan Paul, New York, Knopf, 1937.

DAWSON, Christopher: *Religion and the Rise of Western Culture,* London and New York, Sheed and Ward, 1950.

FLICK, A. C.: *The Decline of the Medieval Church,* London, Kegan Paul, 1930.

GILL, J., S.J.: *The Council of Florence,* Cambridge and New York, Cambridge Univ. Press, 1959.

GUIRAUD, J.: *The Medieval Inquisition* (trans. E. C. Messenger), New York, Benziger, 1929.

HUBER, R. M., O.F.M.: *A Documented History of the Franciscan Order, 1182–1517,* Washington, D.C., Catholic University of America, 1944.

HUGHES, Philip: *A History of the Church:* Volume III, *The Revolt against the Church: Aquinas to Luther,* London and New York, Sheed and Ward, 1947.

• JOINVILLE, Jean de: *History of Saint Louis* (trans. R. Hague), London and New York, Sheed and Ward, 1955.

MACEK, J.: *The Hussite Movement in Bohemia,* Prague, Orbis, 2nd (enlarged) edn, 1958.

Works dealing with philosophy or theology:

ARTZ, F. B.: *The Mind of the Middle Ages*, 2nd edn, New York, Knopf, 1954.

GILSON, Etienne: *The Spirit of Medieval Philosophy*, London, Sheed and Ward, and New York, Scribner, 1936.

LEFF, G.: *Medieval Thought from Saint Augustine to Ockham*, London and Baltimore, Penguin Books, 1958.

The Twentieth Century
Encyclopedia of Catholicism

*The number of each volume indicates
its place in the over-all series
and not the order of publication.*

PART ONE: KNOWLEDGE AND FAITH

PART TWO: THE BASIC TRUTHS

All titles are subject to change.